KILMARTIN

Scotland's richest prehistoric landscape

An Introduction & Guide

by Rachel Butter

with photography by David Lyons

KILMARTIN HOUSE TRUST

Published by Kilmartin House Trust

Second Revised Edition

Kilmartin, Argyll, PA31 8RQ, Scotland

Telephone: 01546 510 278

http://www.kilmartin.org

ISBN 0 9533674 1 X

Supported by the
Heritage Lottery Fund

Designed by James W Murray

Origination by Digital Imaging, Glasgow, Scotland

Printed by Bath Press Colourbooks, Blantyre, Scotland

CONTENTS

*Kilmartin's former manse–now
Kilmartin House Museum–
overlooking the Glebe Cairn, the most northerly of
a line of five cairns stretching across the valley floor*

INTRODUCTION

The inspiration for Kilmartin House Museum, and so for this guide, was the landscape in which the museum is situated. From just outside Kilmartin House one can see a line of burial cairns stretching across the valley, each an example–in its rich and layered history–of the complexities of a past now hidden beneath unpromising piles of stones. Visible too is Upper Largie, now a gravel quarry, a site of human activity over millennia, where people buried their dead, celebrated, mourned and carried out the rituals that made sense of their lives.

A walk behind Kilmartin brings these monuments together and sets them in context. They are not just important in their own right. They are important as part of the wider landscape, which reveals many monuments further and a diversity of landscape forms: one of the last raised peat bogs in Scotland, farmland hard-won, remnant parkland of a Highland estate, estuarine flats and the mountains of the island of Jura in the distance. This landscape, from both a cultural and a natural perspective, is breathtaking.

Yet there is more to understand even than the features picked out from the vantage point above Kilmartin. There are struggles in the landscape, which though not immediately visible to the eye, have inhabited the land from the earliest times, and continue to do so: different perceptions of what the landscape means and what it is for, questions of how it should be used and by whom. These are knitted into its history. Evidence is present for its use as sacred space, shared space, routeway and symbol of power.

No-one has done more than Marion Campbell in studying not just what features in the landscape might have meant to those that built them, but also the meanings which accumulated round about those features. She records stories of standing stones that came to be seen as the graves of Vikings, of fallen monuments used thousands of years later for measuring cloths at cattle fairs, of prehistoric carved rocks being used as Covenanters' altars. We are honoured that she has agreed to add some of her own memories to the beginning of this guide, revealing what these monuments came to mean to her.

Following the important field guide by Marion Campbell and Mary Sandeman, interest in the valley has widened. Many questions,

Carved slab, Nether Largie North Cairn.
Property of National Museums of Scotland.

from the most philosophical to the most practical, are asked of the valley, and many techniques are employed to answer them. Some people seek meaning, others pursue their livelihood, as probably it always has been. We celebrate this diversity of interest, and look forward to the new perspectives and new challenges that lie ahead. We hope too that the study of this landscape in all its facets will bring renewed wisdom and energy in making decisions about its future, difficult though these might be.

Cross-base incised with sundial,
Kilmarie Church, Craignish

ACKNOWLEDGMENTS

This is a museum guide, based on the text at Kilmartin House. It offers no more than an introduction to what is a vast and fascinating subject. Entire books have been written about matters which here are compressed to a page, a paragraph or even a sentence. The footnotes are there to enable people to locate some of these books if they wish–to take their study further and to make up their own minds about important elements of Scotland's history. I have avoided the assumption that the average reader is incapable of tackling works which appear in academic journals. The Further Reading section (p 108) offers some more general suggestions for extending readers' knowledge of specific periods or monument types.

Objects illustrated by colour photographs are on display at Kilmartin House, with the exception of the following: the Irish bowl from the Glebe cairn which alternates between the Museum of Scotland and Kilmartin House, the socketed axe from Loch Glashan, the bird-headed brooch mould and the log boat from Loch Glashan. Objects illustrated by black-and-white photographs or drawings remain with the owning institution. Owners are credited in the text. If no institution is mentioned the object is part of Kilmartin House's own collection.

Photographs and drawings are by David Lyons and Harry Morrison respectively unless another name is given. A name alone refers to the photographer, illustrator or copyright holder of the image. When the acknowledgement refers to ownership of the object rather than the image this is made explicit.

A band of patient and generous spirited academics read over the text in its various stages, answered questions and offered suggestions before the final version was displayed in the museum: John Barrett, Kevin Edwards, Ewan Campbell, Caroline Wickham-Jones. Their knowledge, freely given, was invaluable. Encouragement and help with editing were offered by Helen Butter, David Clough, Donald Farmer, Chris Hudson, Anne Kahane and Lionel Masters. Others who gave advice over specific areas of the text were Mike Davis, Neil Duncan, Murdo McDonald, John Lord and John Purser. Thank you all.

I would also like to thank the visitors to the Museum who took the trouble to point out mistakes they found in the panels.

Information for the timeline was gathered by Damion Willcock. Design work was done by Harry Morrison, with refinements by Chris Hudson and Jimmie Murray. Data was supplied by Paul Buckland, Alastair Dawson, Kevin Edwards, Andrew Kitchener and Richard Tipping. One person's advice sometimes contradicted another's and the result is a compromise - a graphic representation of the problems of attempting a scientific understanding of the past. The only certainty is that in 10 years time our picture of the past will be different.

The colour maps and cover were designed by Martin Gallagher, the former based on maps for the website by Paul Clough.

The main design of the book was by Jimmie Murray, who I thank for his endless patience and encouragement. I would also like to thank Richard Drew for devising a well-structured framework within which to work, and to apologise for ignoring it completely. David Lyons is to be thanked for working well and cheerfully beyond the call of duty, as usual.

Finally I would like to offer thanks and love to David Clough for sharing the delight and inspiration he found in the landscape in which he was brought up. It is a strong landscape, and it changed us both. Let us drink respectfully to that.

FOREWORD

Marion Campbell of Kilberry, FSA Scot. (Hon)

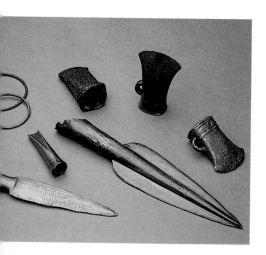

Torran Hoard. *The first part of this hoard was found in 1881. Marion Campbell and Mary Sandeman found the three socketed axes, two rings and a knife in 1962 while conducting the first systematic field survey of ancient monuments in Mid Argyll.*

Here are the keys of a treasure-house, layer upon layer. It is an honour to be asked to write this Foreword, and also a chance to reflect on changes I have seen.

In the early 1950s I was farming and sharing my home with a life-long friend. Our parents had interested us in local history, and we kept meaning to visit the cairns and standing stones we passed on our way to market, if only to fill gaping holes in our knowledge. We made a list, and quickly realised there were far more places on maps than we had noticed, others suggested by place-names, others mentioned in books but unmapped.

Our interest matched those of the new Natural History and Antiquarian Society of Mid Argyll, lately launched by Eric Creegen of happy memory. But to build background knowledge of fact or theory was unbelievably hard. There were few popular books, and the only Archaeology Chair in Scotland was at Edinburgh. Eric found speakers to widen our Mid Argyll horizons, until – in 1963 – I could give a paper to the Society of Antiquaries of Scotland called *Mid Argyll: a Field Survey of the Historic and Prehistoric Monuments* (published in *PSAS* 95).

I view it now with amazement, shame at blunders, and pride. We had recorded 640 sites, measuring most of them, adding a catalogue of finds, four distribution maps, and a graph of heights; it was the product of two untrained women's scanty leisure with a notebook, a six-foot steel tape and a 33-foot surveyor's tape (the largest we could handle on a windy hillside). I doubt if anyone would attempt it now; now one can hardly even park on a roadside and take to the hill as we did then.

We began knowing nothing, trying to educate ourselves; in the end the Society of Antiquaries of Scotland made me an Honorary Fellow. Those were good days, but we never imagined there would be a centre of excellence at Kilmartin as there is now (often as we wished for one), and a book such as this was not in our dreams.

But you, you lucky people, you have it in your hands. May you have as much joy of it as we had of our wanderings!

TIME &
LANDSCAPE

In the landscape surrounding Kilmartin, people have lived, loved, danced, mourned, farmed, hunted, played and prayed for perhaps 10,000 years. This guide looks at how people have used the landscape and how the landscape has affected them.

We will look at the traces people have left behind and at what these say about the struggles, triumphs and achievements that have taken place in Kilmartin Valley. We will also look at natural traces in the landscape – the glacial terraces, the peat bog, the microscopic ancient pollen.

These fragments of the past – the monuments and landscape features we see today, as well as the artefacts, buried settlements and signs of past environments hidden in the ground – tell an intricate story of the relationship between the land and its people.

Kilmartin is a special place. We hope you will find out why this might be.

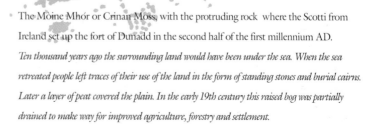

The Moine Mhór or Crinan Moss, with the protruding rock where the Scotti from Ireland set up the fort of Dunadd in the second half of the first millennium AD.

Ten thousand years ago the surrounding land would have been under the sea. When the sea retreated people left traces of their use of the land in the form of standing stones and burial cairns. Later a layer of peat covered the plain. In the early 19th century this raised bog was partially drained to make way for improved agriculture, forestry and settlement.

KILMARTIN'S LANDSCAPE

Scotland was covered by ice from at least 26,000 to 10,000 years ago with a brief warming between 13,500 and 11,000 years ago.[1] It was this ice, and the conditions which followed its melting, which shaped the Kilmartin valley.

The terrace on which the village of Kilmartin stands was formed about 10,000 years ago when water flowed from Loch Awe into the sea at Crinan.[2] This was a wide, fast flowing river, not the tiny burn you see today. Because of later geological changes Loch Awe now discharges its water northwards into Loch Etive.

The last glaciation was one of a series; glaciations happen in cycles. Many occurred before, and many will happen again. We are currently enjoying one of the warm phases when life in the temperate zone happens to be possible. Other warm periods probably lasted in the order of 10-20,000 years, while ours has been continuous for 10,000.[3]

While the structure of the land was being formed by the action of water and ice, life in various forms inhabited its surface. Some of the species of animals and plants which flourished in the extreme conditions of Kilmartin can still be found on Scotland's mountains.

An erratic boulder, *left by the melting ice, perches on a hill above Crinan.*

Koenigia islandica (*Iceland purslane*). Pollen left over
10,000 years ago by this plant was found at Drimnagall,
North Knapdale. Subsequent climatic change caused the
plant to disappear altogether from Argyll, and until recently
it was thought that the nearest place it occurred was Iceland.
Small colonies of the plant, however, are now known to thrive
on Skye and Mull. Michael M Scott.

Diacheila arctica. *Common in the cold late glacial period when it thrived in wet places with sedges, rushes and mosses, this beetle is now rare. It is no longer in Scotland, but is found in Siberia, Russia and Northern Scandinavia.* Painting, Peter Skidmore.

Kilmartin valley with sea (Loch Crinan) in the distance. *The terraces, seen in shadow on the far side of the valley, indicate former sea levels when Kilmartin valley was a tidal estuary.*

Saxifraga oppositifolia *(Purple saxifrage)*
Now present only in Argyll's mountains, these plants flowered thousands of years ago in Kilmartin. Their traces in the form of ancient pollen are preserved in peat and former loch sediment in Ford, Drimnagall and the Mòine Mhór or Moss near Kilmartin. David Whitaker.[4]

Arctic lemming. *The lemming flourished in the western Scottish landscape 10,000 years ago.[5] Its nearest habitat is now Greenland where it eats vegetation such as the roots of tundra plants.* B. Sage.

Carved footprint on Dunadd hill fort. *People have understood the past and the marks it has left in the landscape through legend and storytelling. In the sixteenth century Bishop Carswell, living at Carnassarie Castle, wrote that the people were more interested in stories about the great Irish hero Fionn MacCumhail than in Christianity.[6] This carving was said, in the nineteenth century, to be a trace left by the foot of the legendary Ossian when he leapt across the valley from Rhudil to Dunadd.[7]*

CONSTRUCTING THE PAST

We all play historian, whether by looking at photos, reminiscing, or constructing family trees. Reconstructing the past is an important part of our everyday lives.

Through the past we seek many things: identity, a sense of belonging, lessons for the future. The past has been used in numerous ways– to support nationalist propaganda, to legitimise political regimes, to enhance or damage the status of powerful families.

The time chart overleaf shows 14,000 years of history. To construct it we have used the work of geographers, botanists, historians, archaeologists and geologists. They frequently disagree and we continue to seek refinement and consensus.

Our knowledge is always imperfect and ever-changing; for some, understanding may be more spiritual than scientific.

Chambered Cairn at Nether Largie South, *approx 3,000 BC, showing a cist inserted about 1,000 years later. The reuse of ancient monuments shows people about 4,000 years ago in Kilmartin making connections with the past. The past, represented by the monuments in the landscape, was not ignored, but reviewed, reassessed and revisited.*

HISTORY IN CONTEXT

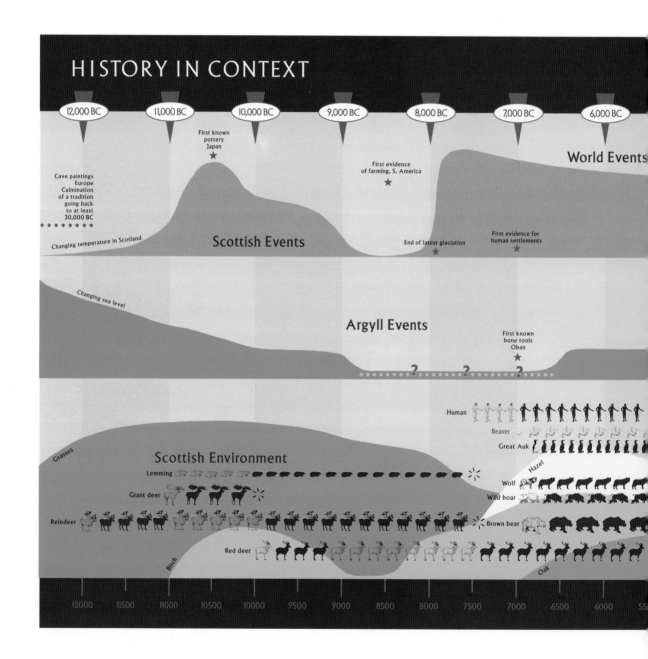

12,000 BC 11,000 BC 10,000 BC 9,000 BC 8,000 BC 7,000 BC 6,000 BC

First known
pottery
Japan
★

First evidence
of farming, S. America
★

World Events

Cave paintings
Europe
Culmination
of a tradition
going back
to at least
30,000 BC

Changing temperature in Scotland

Scottish Events

End of latest glaciation

First evidence for
human settlements
★

Changing sea level

Argyll Events

First known
bone tools
Oban
★

?   ?   ?

Human

Beaver

Great Auk

Hazel

Scottish Environment

Lemming

Wolf

Giant deer

Wild boar

Reindeer

Brown bear

Birch

Red deer

Oak

12000 11500 11000 10500 10000 9500 9000 8500 8000 7500 7000 6500 6000 55

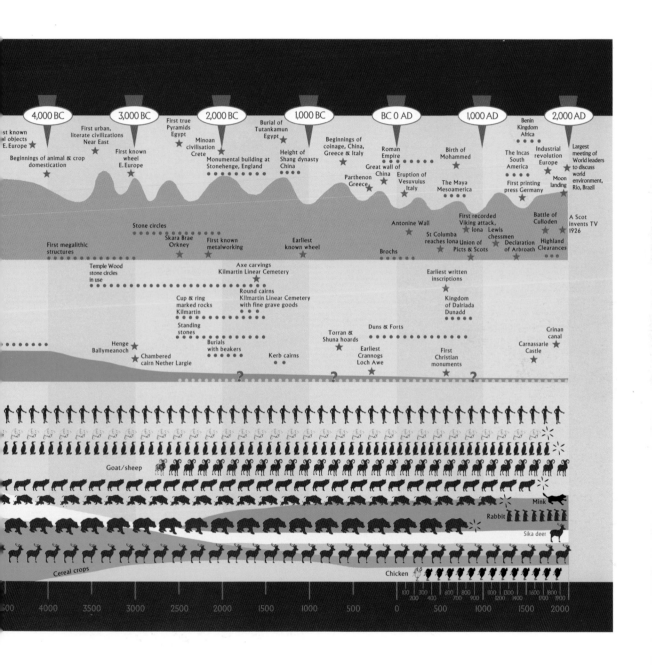

| 4,000 BC | 3,000 BC | 2,000 BC | 1,000 BC | BC 0 AD | 1,000 AD | 2,000 AD |

st known
al objects
E. Europe ★

First urban,
literate civilizations
Near East

First true
Pyramids
Egypt ★

Minoan
civilisation
Crete

Burial of
Tutankamun
Egypt ★

Beginnings of
coinage, China,
Greece & Italy ★

Roman
Empire

Benin
Kingdom
Africa

Largest
meeting of
World leaders
to discuss
world
environment,
Rio, Brazil

Beginnings of animal & crop
domestication ★

First known
wheel
E. Europe ★

Monumental building at
Stonehenge, England ★

Height of
Shang dynasty
China

Great wall of
China

Birth of
Mohammed ★

The Incas
South
America

Industrial
revolution
Europe

Parthenon
Greece ★

Eruption of
Vesuvuius
Italy ★

The Maya
Mesoamerica

First printing
press Germany

Moon
landing

Stone circles

Skara Brae
Orkney ★

First known
metalworking ★

Earliest
known wheel ★

Antonine Wall ★

First recorded
Viking attack,
Iona ★

Battle of
Culloden ★

A Scot
invents TV
1926

First megalithic
structures

St Columba
reaches Iona ★

Union of
Picts & Scots ★

Lewis
chessmen

Declaration
of Arbroath

Highland
Clearances

Brochs ★

Temple Wood
stone circles
in use

Axe carvings
Kilmartin Linear Cemetery ★

Earliest written
inscriptions ★

Cup & ring
marked rocks
Kilmartin

Round cairns
Kilmartin Linear Cemetery
with fine grave goods

Kingdom
of Dalriada
Dunadd ★

Standing
stones

Duns & Forts

Crinan
canal

Henge
Ballymeanoch ★

Burials
with beakers

Torran &
Shuna hoards ★

Carnassarie
Castle ★

Chambered
cairn Nether Largie

Kerb cairns

Earliest
Crannogs
Loch Awe ★

First
Christian
monuments ★

Goat/sheep

Mink

Rabbit

Sika deer

Cereal crops

Chicken

| 500 | 4000 | 3500 | 3000 | 2500 | 2000 | 1500 | 1000 | 500 | 0 | 500 | 1000 | 1500 | 2000 |

see footnotes page 102 for derivation of the data displayed here

TELLING THE TIME

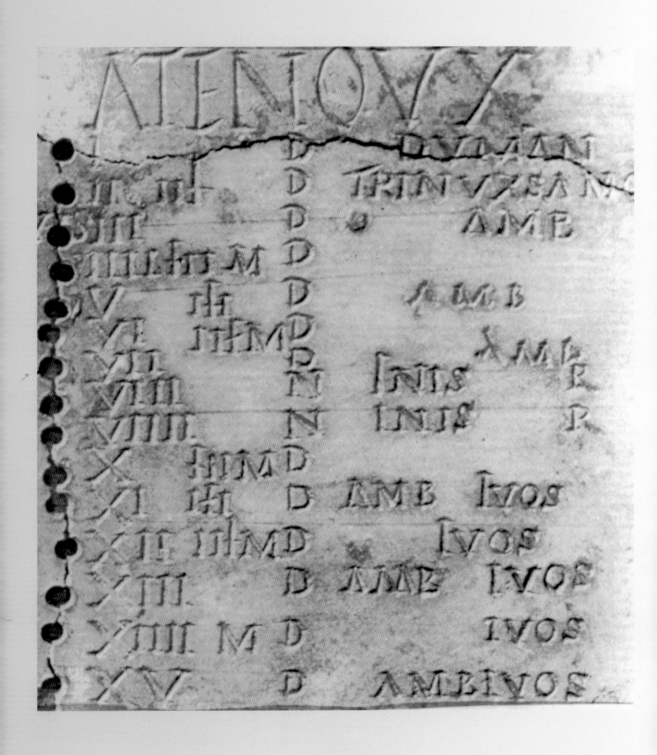

Standing stones at Ballochroy.[8]

Quartz pebbles, Brainport Bay. *Thousands of years ago people left a pile of 33 quartz pebbles in a neat cluster at a prehistoric site on Loch Fyne. The site is directed towards sunrise on the midsummer solstice and the excavator suggested that these stones may have been counters used in some way as an aid for recording the passing of time.*[9]

Gaulish calendar, Coligny. *The Celts in France made this calendar in the 1st century BC, drawing on detailed knowledge of the movement of the sun and moon. Roman writers report that northern Celts had sophisticated knowledge of both solar and lunar cycles.* Christian Thioc, Musée de la Civilisation gallo-romaine, Lyon, France.[10]

Orientating ourselves in time remains a significant human preoccupation. We celebrate birthdays and anniversaries and diligently observe the turning of the year, century and millennium.

The construction of calendars to enable precision in such celebrations is an ancient and enduring endeavour.[11] One of the most influential debates in church history, for example, was about when to celebrate Easter–not roughly but precisely.[12]

Some of Kilmartin's prehistoric monuments may represent the same struggle to fix time accurately, by reference to the movement of the sun and moon.[13] This goes beyond the purely practical requirements of a farming society, however complex.

The earliest people of Argyll knew where they were in time by observing changes in the landscape and sky, and by noticing the behaviour of animals and plants. Today we can measure time in nanoseconds and eras. The landscape, however, with its monuments, its layers of history, and its memories, is still the most important means we have of giving a sense of age and depth to our existence–of orientating ourselves in time.

SEEING THE LANDSCAPE

What people value in the landscape depends on who they are and when they live. The flat expanse of bog–the Mòine Mhór or Moss– stretching from Crinan to Kilmartin has at different times been valued for its spiritual, scientific, recreational, and economic qualities.

People's feelings about the landscape are coloured additionally by their attitude towards monuments. A person who believes standing stones are war memorials sees a different landscape from the person who thinks they are part of a calendar or the source of spiritual energies.

What people see in the landscape also depends on what they remember.

The memory of a brave, brutal or compassionate act lives on in the landscape–in the clearing or by the stone or stream crossing where the deed took place. War leaves many such imprints in the landscape.

The landscape changes as memories are forgotten, and new ones take their place. It looks different to the person who knows the landscape and its stories than to the person who does not.

The Mòine Mhór or Moss has been celebrated by different people for many different reasons:

'If the moss at Crinan were improved, it will make a beautiful plain, as the crops I saw on the parts already cleared were exceeding good.' J Robson in General view of Agriculture in the County of Argyll, 1794.

'A naturalist and sportsman may be permitted to regret the utilitarian proceeding which turned the greater part of an ideal snipe bog into indifferent farms.' The Hon. A E Gathorne-Hardy, Autumns in Argyllshire with Rod and Gun, 1901.

'This area is one of the most important bog sites, or more accurately raised mire sites, in Britain today...One of the major points of interest about the Mòine Mhór is the transition in vegetation from the central acid raised mire to the salt marsh down by the coast with a range of communities in between.' Dave Batty, Scottish Natural Heritage, 1993.

'...the Mòine Mhór may be one of the best localities in western Scotland for dating mid and late Flandrian sea-level change.' Haggart and Sutherland in Quaternary Research Association's Field Guide to the South-West Scottish Highlands, 1992.

Island, Loch Leathan. *This is one of several landmarks near Kilmartin that came to be associated with the violence and loss of the 17th century covenanting wars. It is alleged that this island was a refuge, and that as the army led by Alexander McDonald marched past, a local man defiantly fired an arrow which killed the leader's right hand man.*[14]

Kilmartin Valley *with Loch Awe visible at the top right.* *Kilmartin's strategic position between sea and lochs helped to give it importance throughout prehistory. Even as recently as 1794 an agricultural surveyor remarks –'The convenience of water carriage, exempts the people in Argyleshire, from the absolute necessity of an expensive attention to roads.'* J Robson in General View of Agriculture in the County of Argyll, 1794.

Temple Wood circles, Nether Largie Stones and Nether Largie South chambered cairn in fields on the valley floor. *Aerial photographs can show marks in the ground that are not visible from the surface.*

Standing stones, Mòine Mhór. *It is difficult to pick out features in the landscape which can be said without doubt to be the result solely of natural climate change. Peat forms when the climate is wet, so we can say that the growth of peat over prehistoric monuments was the result of deteriorating climate. It is possible, however, for people to create the conditions which accelerate this process.*[15]

In Kilmartin's landscape we can see examples of some of the natural processes and many of the human actions that have shaped and continue to shape the environment in which we live. Though parts of the landscape may seem wild and unspoilt, every inch of land surrounding Kilmartin has been affected, either directly or indirectly, by people.

In some cases people have manipulated the landscape deliberately to create something new and different. The construction, 4,000 years ago, of the linear cemetery several kilometres long, and the draining of the Moss 200 years ago are both visionary schemes, carefully planned.[16]

In other cases changes in the landscape have not been planned. The lack of heather and native trees on the hills is the result of an increase in grazing by sheep. The dominance of commercial non-native forestry around Kilmartin is part of a nationwide trend to increase wood production. Visually such changes have a profound impact on the landscape.[17]

Temple Wood. Engraving by William Daniell, 1817

In the early 19th century an ambitious project aimed to drain and strip the extensive peat bog around Kilmartin and use the land for agriculture; people removing peat can be seen to the right. In the process the remains of a former project which had also transformed the landscape were revealed.

The stone circle and cairn are some of the earliest monuments in the evolution of a powerful ritual landscape, which both celebrated and helped to maintain the spiritual qualities of the valley between about 3,500 and 1,500 BC.[18]

Standing stones (fallen), Dunamuck.

These stones are the survivors of a group of monuments that around 4,000 years ago included at least two stone circles and possibly a ceremonial avenue. Thousands of years later many such monuments lay covered in peat and apparently forgotten.

Later, Dunamuck's strategic position, and perhaps memories of its former ceremonial status, led people to use it for the great Kilmichael Tryst, an important fair and market to which cattle traders came from all over Scotland. On these occasions people used the ancient stones - some now fallen - to measure pieces of cloth.[19]

Abandoned village of Brenphort. *In 1314 Robert the Bruce gave the lands around Kilmartin to Sir Colin Campbell in return for 'a ship of 40 oars with sufficient men and furniture for 40 days, and the other service wont to be paid by the barons of Argyyle'.[20] For the king, who under the feudal system owned all the land in Scotland, the value of a piece of land was not simply that it produced crops, minerals or wood, but that it produced people too.*

More recently the human component of the landscape has been less valued. Where once people lived and worked, bracken now invades.

Portion of General Roy's map, 1748. *The landscape shown in this map was still dominated by the peat bogs which had been forming for at least 2,000 years. The area is described in 1793 as 'distant from the scenes of great and memorable events, backward in most kinds of improvements, particularly in agriculture, and without trade or manufactures'.[21] All was to change with the agricultural improvements of the early 19th century.* British Library.

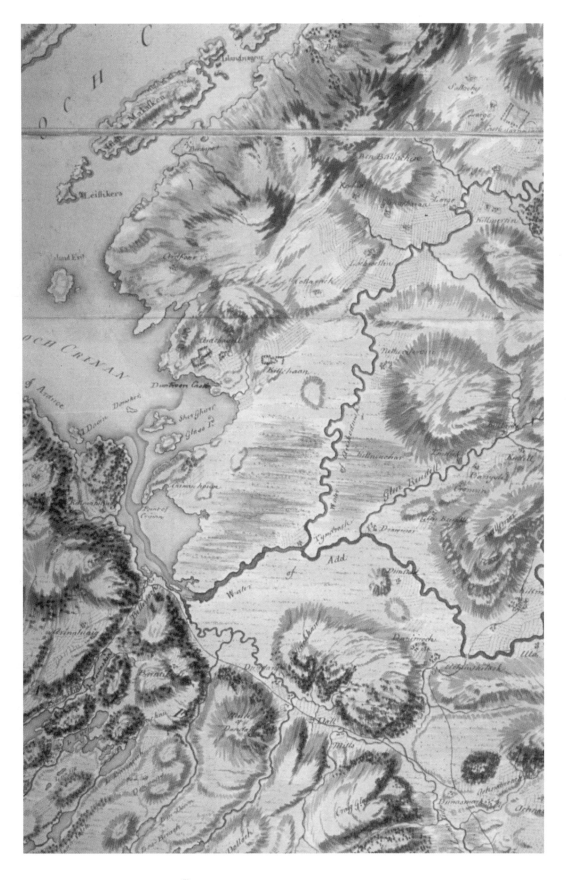

Crinan Moss showing drained and undrained fields, with Poltalloch mansion house in the background. [22]
The draining of the Moss was not just an economic scheme for increasing the productivity of the land. It represented the height of human domination of the landscape and was accompanied by other grand statements which proclaimed the power and prestige of its architect - a spectacular mansion, seen in the background, and grand park land aesthetically planted.

Commercial forestry.

There are now many more non-native trees in the area than native
species. Until last century native trees were planted for commercial
reasons, but now Sitka spruce and other fast-growing Scandinavian
trees are considered the ones most profitable. An 1816 recommendation
for the planting of oaks (whose bark was used for tanning) near
Kilmartin takes both the economic and visual into account, remarking
that 'they will form one whole forest of wood, and will have a most
imposing and beautiful effect - besides considering it as a profitable
concern'. Poltalloch papers.[23]

Gravel quarry, Kilmartin.

This landscape has been valued in several opposing ways. The gravel terraces were attractive to people over 4,000 years ago:[24] *here they buried their dead and perhaps enacted the ceremonies which gave meaning to their lives. Recently the same terrace has been valued by some people as a source of gravel for building and a commercial resource, and by others as a source of information on how people lived in the past.*[25]

Aerial view of Nether Largie North cairn.[26] *The landscape today is divided into compartments. The cairns of the Linear Cemetery, once united, are now neatly cordoned off and the land round about is owned in separate parcels.*

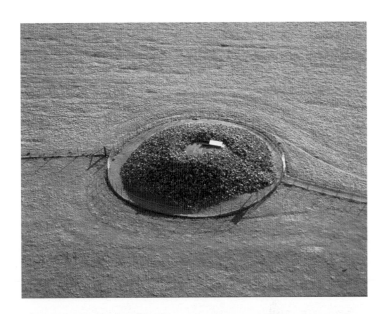

Craignish chapel.[27] *The position of monuments in relation to the movement of the sun and moon had a greater importance in prehistory than today. Perhaps it was a memory of this relationship between the land, the sky, and the religious monument that meant that as late as 1650 the parishioners of Craignish were rebuked by the Kirk Session for 'goeing sungates about the church before they go in to the kirk for divyne service'.* Minutes of Argyll Synod, 1650.[28]

Portion of Blaeu map, 1646.

The landscape which this map depicts was deeply affected by civil war. The parish of Glassary was described as 'desolat of people and altogether destitute of maintenance...'. Among many concerns were 'the appearance of famine by the late harvest and hard weather and so many armies on foot, who (if God pity not the land) will eat up the substance thereof shortly'. Minutes of Argyll Synod, 1646 & 1650. [29]

Carnassarie Castle.[30]

Carnassarie Castle holds memories of a time when the landscape was one of terror. Members of opposing factions lived in neighbouring farms, and people's livelihoods - their cattle, sheep and horses - could be seized on the slightest pretext.

A petition to parliament on behalf of Duncan of Auchinbreck, who lost his holding of the castle because of the part he played in an uprising against the king in 1685 [31], describes 'all imaginable cruelty, rapine, violence and oppression committed on his near relations, friends, vassals, and tenants; and after capitulation and assurance given, no faith kept; his friends killed and hanged at his gates; his houses burnt to ashes, all the goods secured by said assurance, robbed and taken away, – all other unparalleled barbarities committed …'[32]

At least 43 inhabitants of Kilmartin parish lost goods on account of the part they played (many reluctantly) in the rebellion. The total number of animals seized from Kilmartin parish was 177 cows, 14 horses, 7 mares and 5 sheep.[33]

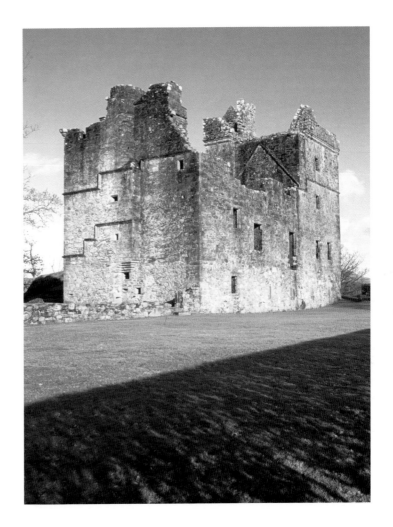

Shielings on Jura,

from Pennant's Tour in Scotland, 1772.

The introduction of farming 6,000 years ago did not lead to completely settled lives. People have almost always occupied different bits of the landscape according to the season. Pennant describes these as the 'summer huts' of herders who kept a flock of 80 goats for milk and cheese. They 'formed a grotesque groupe; some were oblong, many conic, and so low that entrance is forbidden, without creeping through the little opening, which has no other door than a faggot of birch twigs, placed there occasionally: they are constructed of branches of trees, covered with sods; the furniture a bed of heath, placed on a bank of sod; two blankets and a rug; some dairy vessels, and above, certain pendent shelves made of basket work, to hold the cheese, the produce of the Summer'.[34]

CLOSE TO THE WIND

The landscape which Argyll's first people moved into was dramatically different from that of today. It required a completely different strategy for living.

Nearly 8,000 years ago someone on the isle of Colonsay left the remains of thousands of burnt hazelnut shells. On the shore beside Oban someone discarded an antler harpoon, and on the island of Jura people were making implements using tiny pieces of flint. These are some of the first traces of human occupation in Argyll. [1]

At the time when these remains were left, Jura was cloaked in birch and Kilmartin was wooded with birch, hazel, oak and elm. The sea level was lower than it is today. [2]

A thousand years later the sea was at its highest, reaching almost as far as Kilmartin. The weather was probably warmer and slightly wetter than today. People have left traces of a complex economy on Argyll's coast at this time–the oysters and shellfish they ate, the antler and stone they used to make tools, the tiny shells they used to adorn themselves.

These traces show an intelligent, imaginative and dextrous group of people, living in a landscape which presented both opportunity and challenge. Their lives were shaped by Argyll's naturally evolving landscape and they used it in complex ways we don't fully understand.

CROSSING THE WATER

The earliest known depiction of a boat
is this 10,000 year old carving in Norway.[3]

Reconstruction of an 18th century coracle found near the
River Spey.[4]

The earliest carbon dated boat in Scotland - a log boat - is over 4,000 years old,[5] but people in Scotland needed boats long before this. The earliest inhabitants of Argyll's coast used boats to get around, to transport material and to fish.[6]

It is likely that these boats were made from skin and wicker. The tools which people left in caves in Oban and on the islands of Oronsay, Colonsay and Jura show they had the necessary technology–flints for preparing hides, awls for piercing, needles for sewing and blades for cutting hazel or willow.

A Roman writer reports the use of skin boats around British waters in the 6th century BC: [7]

> *They know not to fit with pine*
> *Their keels, nor with fir, as use is,*
> *They shape their boats; but strange to say,*
> *They fit their vessels with united skins,*
> *And often traverse the deep in a hide.*

Such boats are quick to make, light to carry, and much more seaworthy than the log boat. People used them in Scotland up to the eighteenth century, and still use them today in Wales and Ireland.

Besides the skills necessary to make the boat, people required a sophisticated understanding of the moon and tides in order to voyage safely in the waters around Kilmartin, some of the most powerful tidal streams in Europe.[8]

MAKING BOATS

Wicker and hide boats are elegantly simple, and quick to make. Their size depends on the number and size of hides available. Straight thin wands of hazel are stuck in the ground, outlining the form (a). Bent over and lashed fast with gut and fibre, they are strengthened with woven willow to create the frame (b). Uprooted and reversed it becomes a wicker hull (c). Soggy hides, sewn to size, are secured and left to dry and tighten (d). A final water-proofing with seal oil and it is ready to catch the next favourable tide.[9]

(a)

(b)

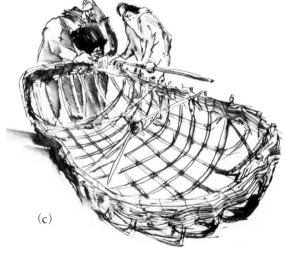

(c)

(d)

Sound of Jura. *We don't know where the earliest settlers came from but, shaped by the landscape, they soon developed a collection of tools and ways of living peculiar to Scotland's west coast.*[10]

LIVING FROM THE SHORE

There was plenty of food in the seas and forests of Argyll. The earliest people left abundant evidence of their success in harvesting it.

On Oronsay they dined on at least 23 species of fish, 30 species of birds, plus oysters and crab - now considered delicacies–and various other shellfish such as limpets and whelk. They made adornments from cowrie shells, containers from scallop shells and they prized the soft pelt of the otter. They fashioned barbed points, awls and mattocks from antler and bone, which they collected by boat from bigger islands or the mainland. People on Risga– an island in Ardnamurchan– and in Oban left very similar traces.[11]

These remains provide just one window into the complex lives of these people. Sites on Jura and Islay, with different sorts of evidence, provide another. There the remains are predominantly flint, with over 1,500 pieces from one site on Jura alone.[12]

There are few clues to aspects of life beyond the seeking of food and shelter. The spiritual side of people's lives was not expressed in the kind of durable monument which later generations of farmers were to build. For Argyll's earliest settlers the whole landscape may have been sacred, and needed no lasting monuments. They may have celebrated the links between the moon, the tides and the cycle of their lives, but such rituals have left no traces.

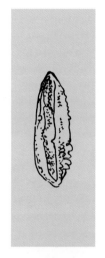

Otolith. *It is possible to say at what time of year the fish saithe was caught by measuring its otolith or ear bone. Measurement and comparison of thousands of such otoliths from various shell middens on Oronsay, together with other data, enabled the excavator to compile the map shown below. It shows the shell middens and their main season of occupation.* Map by Paul Mellars.

Human finger bone, Cnoc Coig, Oronsay. *There are no formal burials from the pre-farming period in Argyll, but a few human bones from the shell midden - all fingers and toes - hint at some kind of burial rite. The detail, motivation and ceremony of such a rite we can only imagine. The shape of this bone suggests strong muscular attachments, indicating that the person had a firm grip.* Paul Mellars.[13]

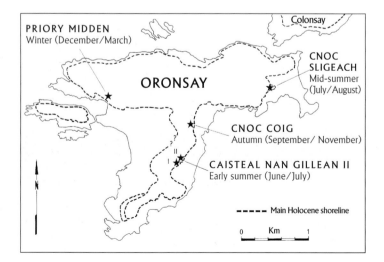

PRIORY MIDDEN
Winter (December/March)

Colonsay

CNOC SLIGEACH
Mid-summer (July/August)

ORONSAY

CNOC COIG
Autumn (September/November)

CAISTEAL NAN GILLEAN II
Early summer (June/July)

- - - - Main Holocene shoreline

0   Km   1

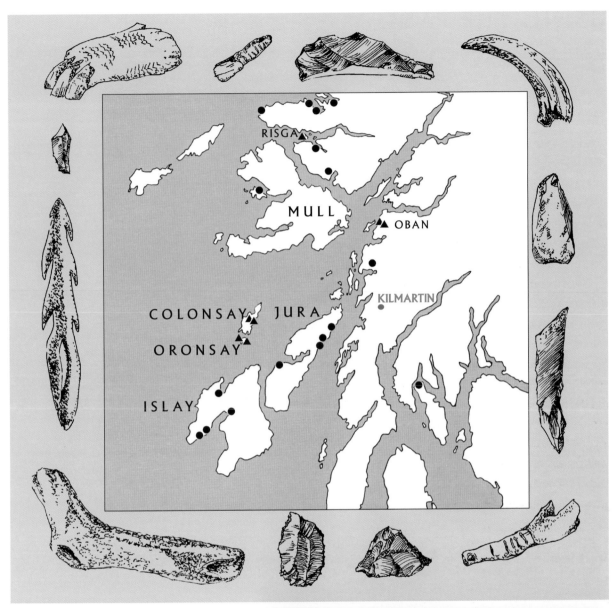

RISGA ▲
MULL
▲ OBAN
KILMARTIN
COLONSAY ▲ JURA
ORONSAY ▲▲
ISLAY

Almost all the evidence from the pre-farming period in Argyll has been found on the coast. If there were sites inland they would be difficult to detect today as farming quickly destroys the few traces which nomadic people leave. Sites where bone implements such as barbed points were found are marked ▲ other early sites are marked ●.

Perforated cowrie shell , Cnoc Sligeach, Oronsay. Property of Hunterian Museum, Glasgow.

Antler harpoons. *Barbed points have been found on Argyll's early coastal sites, some of bone, some of antler. People may have used them as harpoon heads, as suggested in the reconstructions shown here.*

USING THE PAST

Landscape features such as Caisteal nan Gillean (see below) provided obvious targets for 19th century antiquarians. The quality of the excavations often depended on the personal quests of the chief investigator. Some were interested simply in the recovery of impressive objects, others sought to throw light on the controversial issues of the day regarding human evolution and the formation and antiquity of the Earth.[14]

Later investigators focused more on detail. They searched for collections of artefacts that might represent the activities of a distinct group of people. The harpoons and bone implements of Oban, Oronsay and Risga, for example, were said to be the products of the 'Obanian' people. [15] Today the investigator's search is even more detailed.

The recent excavations on Oronsay comprised six seasons of work between 1970 and 79, and work towards the specialist reports is still, in 1998, underway. [16] There is detailed information on fish, birds, snails, shells, stones, bones and pollen. From this mass of data a picture is sought of the economic, social and environmental background to Scotland's early settlers.

Great Auk. *Symington Grieve excavated Caisteal nan Gillean in the 1880s. He hoped to find burials in the mound but, finding none, became more interested in the animal remains, in particular the bones of the Great Auk which had only recently become extinct. He was relatively uninterested in the artefacts, and several pieces, which we would now consider important, were lost.* [18] © Trustees of the National Museums of Scotland (photograph and object owned by NMS).

Dog whelk. *The detailed statistical analyses employed in the most recent excavations on Oronsay included the measurement of hundreds of both prehistoric and present-day dog whelk shells. The ratio of aperture length to total shell length alters according to the severity of wind. Through such data an idea is sought of the weather conditions for Oronsay's prehistoric inhabitants. Evidence from the dog whelk and botanical data suggests that the climate was milder and less windy than it is today.* [19]

Caisteal nan Gillean. *This shell mound consists of thousands of discarded shells, built up over hundreds of years from 5,100 to 4,300 BC.* Society of Antiquaries of Scotland.[17]

REV. J. HUTCHISON ON THE CAVE.

On Sabbath evening last Rev. James Hutchison, M.A., delivered a most impressive sermon to young men, on "Lessons from the Cave," in the Oban U.P. Church. The church was well filled, and the preacher was listened with marked attention throughout. Taking for his text 1 John ii. 17—"The world passeth away and the lust thereof, but he that doeth the will of God abideth forever," the rev. gentleman began by saying that it is a twice told tale that the world is passing away; all things are in flux, nothing abides. The generation of men are like the generation of the leaves, and the solid land and the shore-bound sea have their epochs of change no less wonderful. As a community our thoughts had been turned forcibly to these facts by the discovery of the cave-dwelling which Dr Anderson of Edinburgh had declared to be the most important yet discovered in Scotland. After a brief description of the cave and its contents, the speaker went on to say that the question of date was one for speculation and not for true science. Archæology knows no dates, and when it attempts a chronology it is shorn of its strength. It deals with condition and sequence, but not with date. At the same time Dr Anderson, in conversation on the subject, had admitted that the very latest possible date for even the upper stratum was 400 or 500 years B.C. The rev. gentleman then proceeded to say that the pulpit was not the place for dwelling exclusively on the scientific lessons taught by the cave, but he wished to emphasise the fact that the cave, now 48 feet above sea level, was once on that level, and that the change was due to a rise of the land, and not, as many seemed to suppose, to a receding of the sea. In answer to the question "What can we learn from the cave as to man's place in nature? The speaker affirmed that while in no way anxious to disprove the Darwinian theory of Ape descent, the evidence of this cave, and of all other similar discoveries, showed no approximation to a pre-human type. It was negative evidence no doubt, but geology so far had not supported Darwin. Further, the pre-historic men were tool-using creatures, and this marked them off from the highest animals; the latter modified themselves by thickening their fur, etc., whereas man modified his environment. The rev. gentleman then asked if we were to conclude that man, who was the highest of the creatures, passed away for ever like the sun sinking at mid-day, and examined the testimony of men of science as to the probability of immortality. Real science, therefore, did not conflict with Christian belief in immortality, but men of the highest eminence deduced it from their own conclusions in physics. The speaker, at considerable length, applied the truth "He that doeth the will of God abideth for ever." The only abiding thing was the character a man made for himself. When the palm branch on the soldier's brow had withered, and the name had been bitten by the frost off the rich man's tombstone, and the university roll of honour had crumbled, a man's true self would be fresh and youthful.

THE OBAN CAVE DISCOVERY.

[TO THE EDITOR OF THE "OBAN TIMES."]

Oban Times, 1895. *Archaeology had the potential to throw light on the age of the world, and mankind's place and development within it. Since the publication in 1859 of Darwin's* Origin of Species *these were increasingly important and controversial subjects for everyone from scientist to priest. The Oban excavations were reported regularly in the Oban Times, finds were displayed in the ironmonger's shop as they were discovered, and a lecture on the moral lessons to be gleaned from the excavations was delivered to a full hall.* [20]

THE RED DEER

This important source of so many items of subsistence may also have provided inspiration for celebration and worship. Some antlers found in Yorkshire may support this idea–they are perforated at the base as if worn as a head-dress.[21] Depictions of strange figures, part deer, part human, go back a long way–to Palaeolithic France and Iron Age Italy. A god with antlers is shown on a silver cauldron from Denmark dating to around 200 BC.[22] The Celts worshipped a deity which could take on the form of a deer, and in Anglo-Saxon Britain the people prayed to Herne the Hunter, the horned god.

In Denmark 6,000 years ago, a woman and child were laid in a grave, the child lying on a swan's wing. A man in the same place went to his grave with a set of antlers.[23]

People would be thrifty in the way they used such a precious resource as the red deer, and each deer would be used differently according to which items were needed at the time. A single large stag could, for example, provide the things listed opposite.

CLOSE TO THE WIND ✕

As well as the barbed points, needles and awls which could be extracted from the main beam of the antlers, the tines or points could be used as punches, piercers and flint-working tools. The thickness of some early antler remains show that prehistoric animals were larger than those found in Scotland today.

This exhibit shows from which part of the antler various tools could be made. It has been made by a modern craftsman using only flint tools and fire.

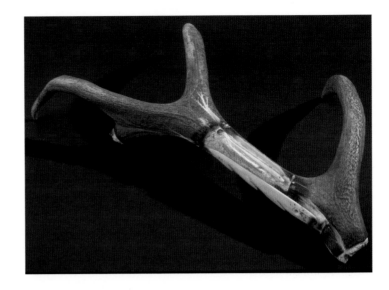

✕ enough skin to cover a small coracle or to make a tunic and a pair of shoes

✕ several barbed points which could be used as harpoon or spear heads

✕ a bundle of needles for stitching clothing, skin boats and netting

✕ a mattock which could be used for digging, or for butchering.

✕ a support for a bow drill

✕ a pressure flaker for fine flint work

✕ several tooth picks

✕ enough calories in the meat to feed a family group of 3 adults and 2 children for two weeks

✕ 60cm of tough sinew cordage

✕ 10m of twisted gut cordage

✕ fat and hoof oil for a lamp

✕ bone awls, skin rubbing tools, punches and toggles

✕ a tooth necklace

✕ brain for tanning the hide

✕ ceremonial head-dress from the skull

✕ three containers for carrying liquid, made from the stomach, the bladder and the large intestine.

An incantation is made to the deer,
the provider of food, tools, and clothing.

THE WOOD AGE

While the sea was at its highest levels and the coastal waters provided a healthy marine diet, the forest of Mid Argyll presented a different, rich and varied environment.[24]

There may have been light open areas, but the forest was big enough and dense enough to get lost in. It contained massive oak trees, hazel, elm and birch. It provided food, fuel, clothing, shelter and inspiration.

Like the sea the forest was an environment which held dangers as well as riches. But to those who knew it, it was a friend. It was a landscape alive with sounds no longer familiar in Kilmartin–the sounds of the wolf and boar, and a chorus of bird song.[25]

This is the age of wood as much as of stone. For every microlith there is a haft, for every arrowhead a shaft.[26] Special places were marked not by stone monuments, but by natural features in the landscape: ancient trees, clearings, stream crossings, pathways. The forest would contain both ancient landmarks, and signs of change.

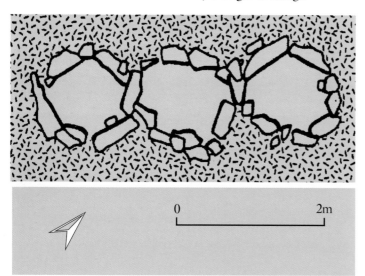

0   2m

Stone settings found at Lussa Wood *on the isle of Jura, could be the remains of an early settlement site, or perhaps they are where people built fires and cooked food. The site dates to around 6,000 BC.*[27]

Alan Braby. Crown copyright reproduced courtesy of Historic Scotland.

Water lily. *Plants other than trees were important. Sedges, grasses and iris could be used to make baskets, nettle leaves could be eaten and nettle fibres used to make cordage. The edible seeds of the water lily were found on an early site in the north of Ireland.*[28]

MOVING THROUGH THE LANDSCAPE

People may have visited Kilmartin only for short stays, to catch salmon in the Add perhaps, or to hunt for wild boar. Or they may have settled for longer periods. We can only guess at the routes they might have taken–along water courses or following forest paths. No trace of their occupation remains.

The early settlers moved across huge areas of the land and various habitats. Their intimate knowledge of wide territories allowed them to adapt to changes. Small groups needed to be in contact with others, perhaps distant, to find marriage partners for example, so meeting areas would have been very important. Special places in the landscape must have existed even before people started to mark them with monuments.

Approximately 6,000 years ago, people began to create permanent settlements and to grow their own food. The forest then presented a new face, for although it remained a vital resource it was also an obstacle to the first farmers.[31]

Rock shelter, Crinan Ferry. *There are many caves on the coast of Argyll, some of which may have been used for temporary shelter by the earliest settlers. More recent use has often destroyed any traces of ancient habitation, but at Crinan Ferry some prehistoric pottery was found.*[29]

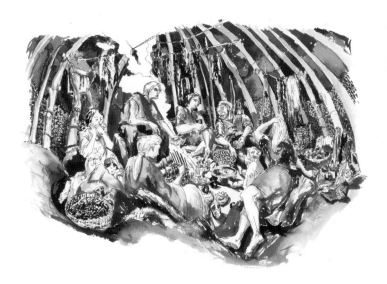

The inside of a tent made from wood and animal skins could be warm and comfortable.

Boar's tusk, Druimvargie rock shelter, Oban. *People on the coast relied on products of the woodland too. This tusk was found with tools of deer bone and the remains of shellfish in a coastal rock shelter used around 8,000 years ago.*[30]
Property of Argyll and Bute Museums Service.

BREAKING THE EARTH

We know very little about the beginnings of farming in Kilmartin. It probably made little impact on the landscape at first. Ultimately it had the profoundest effect of all. Early agriculture in Scotland is traditionally associated with permanent settlement, the adoption of pottery, woodland clearance and the introduction of new plant and animal species. Not enough evidence has yet been found in Kilmartin about any of these.

The earliest traces of a settled agricultural community in Argyll are at Ardnadam, near Dunoon. People lived there from around 3,700 BC. They built small round-cornered houses of turf, stone and stakes, and used polished stone axes and pottery.[1] Meanwhile, near Oban and on Oronsay people living a different sort of life were continuing to contribute to the build-up of shell middens.[2]

We don't know where in the Kilmartin valley, if anywhere, people lived. The clues here are of a different sort. Rather than settlements, the earliest sites are ceremonial such as a wooden structure at Temple Wood–possibly a solar observatory.[3]

Clay daub and carbonised hazel, Bruach an Druimein. *Some stone foundations, post holes and pits are the only clues we presently have to early habitation in the Kilmartin valley. A circular oak-framed building once stood on the site. Pits nearby contained barley and oat grains, shells and remnants of wattle and daub wall construction. For this technique people created a frame from interwoven wands of wood which they then plastered with a mixture containing clay and lime.*[4] Property of Glasgow Museums: Art Gallery and Museum Kelvingrove.

Section through field boundaries, Connel, near Oban. ▶
Before 1,500 BC some people in northern Argyll built at least 72 metres of low turf and stone walling. They constructed it carefully, with boulders making up the faces, and earth and small stones used as a filling. The landscape at the time was open heath land. It was no longer thickly forested and its relatively few trees consisted mostly of alder.

About 1,500 BC peat began to accumulate, eventually blanketing the site in a layer 1.5m thick. The excavators suggest that the agricultural practices themselves may have accelerated this peat growth. G & A Ritchie.[5] Reproduced courtesy of Glasgow Archaeological Society.

Plan of settlement site, Ardnadam, Argyll. *This mass of* ▶ *post holes represents five structures, one of which was carbon dated to about 3,700 BC. Evidence for the use and reuse of the site made the excavation director think that herdsmen may have used the site, on a seasonal rather than permanent basis. Pollen analysis also indicated that pastoral rather than arable farming may have predominated at this time.* Betty Rennie. Reproduced courtesy of Glasgow Archaeological Society.

Ard marks, Machrie Moor, Arran. About 2,000 BC. ▶ *These scratches in the ground show us where, about 4,000 years ago, people turned the soil over using a light plough or ard. They grew barley, and may have manured their fields using seaweed and bracken. This is suggested by traces of algal spores, bracken fronds and cereal pollen found in the ancient layer of soil.*[6] Alison Haggerty. Reproduced courtesy of Historic Scotland.

MAKING MARKS

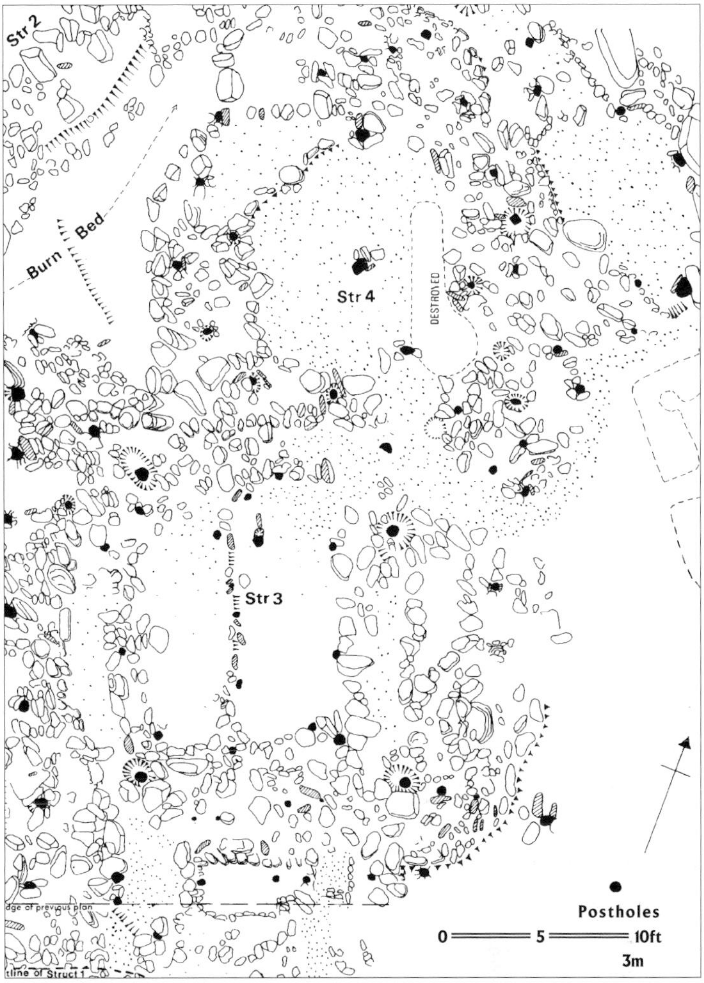

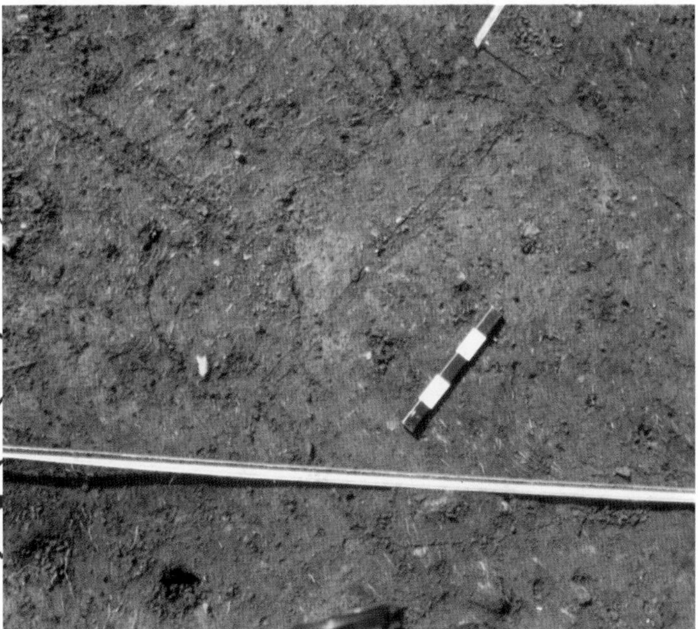

Str 2

Burn Bed

Str 4

DESTROYED

Str 3

Postholes

0 ===== 5 ===== 10ft

3m

edge of previous plan

line of Struct 1

HUNTING FOR NEW WAYS

Kilmartin's early farmers may have been primarily herdsmen and shepherds, whose existence was not completely static. Nevertheless farming did lead to a less mobile life.

The insecurities accompanying a life on the move were replaced by new concerns. The building of monuments is one endeavour which has left significant traces around Kilmartin. Here at least seven stone burial cairns with chambers dominated the landscape.[7]

The customs and activities practised in Kilmartin over the 3,000 years prior to farming did not die. A leaf shaped arrowhead found in the soil is a sign that someone, perhaps 5,000 years ago, was out hunting. Hunting continued, though its role has gradually changed from a significant means of survival to the expensive and ritualised activity we know today.

Leaf arrowhead (replica).

Even farmers hunt. *Here the artist imagines a ceremonial prehistoric hunting expedition. The hunt enables people to show off their prowess, to bond with their fellows, and perhaps to encircle and overpower their prey. In this case the prey is the legendary wild boar.* [8]

We do not know exactly when people started to plough the fields around Kilmartin. If they were doing so 4,000 years ago the scene was perhaps as we show here. People are plough-ing the fields around Dunadd - the peat had not yet formed. They are using both human power and the power of oxen, yoked together.

STATUS FROM STONE

Wood was still the most important material for tools, weapons, fuel and containers but stone was sharp and heavy and had specific uses.

Stone was also distinctive and sometimes beautiful. People could use exotic or special stone to show off, and would go to some lengths to acquire it. Although attractive, some axes were too fragile to be used while others were too big or too small. Of 22 stone axes tested from Argyll, seven were made of Irish stone and five of stone from Cumbria.[10] These axes changed hands as rare and valuable objects.

Kilmartin is not rich in stones suitable for tool-making. Flint pebbles could be picked up on the beach, but they were small and difficult to use. The nearest source of large flints was Antrim, 20 miles from Argyll on the Irish coast. An alternative was pitchstone, a volcanic glass from Arran.

Quartz is abundant in Kilmartin and may have been used to make tools. It shatters rather than flakes, making it difficult to tell if it has been worked or not. Quartz is often found in graves and scattered over cairns, suggesting a decorative, purifying or hallowing use.[11] Even today quartz is believed to have an energising effect.

Polished stone axes and carved balls. *The axe from Poltalloch Estate (left) is probably made from material imported from northern Ireland.*[12] *The one from Creag Ghlas (right) is reported in 1865 as being one of several large flints and stone hatchets. Perhaps it was part of a hoard. Stone could make efficient cutting tools other than axes. The shape of the implement from Drimvore (middle) suggests it was mounted at right angles to the usual cutting edge and may have been used as a chisel.*

The function of carved stone balls is not known. Almost 400 have been found, all but 5 in Scotland. People in the village of Skara Brae on the Orkney Islands used them over 4,000 years ago. The balls shown here, from Castle Sween and the early historic fort of Dunadd, may have been brought to these sites thousands of years after they were made.

All the property of National Museums of Scotland.

◀ Flint axes, Auchenhoan. *These axes, found together in Kintyre, are made of flint from Ireland. They date to between 4,000 and 3,000 BC.* [13]
© Property of the National Museums of Scotland. Objects owned by NMS.

Arrows *were practical items, but many stone arrowheads are made more carefully than was necessary, suggesting they had a special value. The replicas show three different styles used at different periods in prehistory.* [14]

Chambered cairn, near Kilmartin c 3,000 BC. The use of stone in construction had a striking effect both on the landscape and on those who inhabited it. [15]

VESSELS FROM THE EARTH

Once broken, turned and planted the earth brought forth crops. Some of these, and many wild plants such as honeysuckle, iris and sedge, could be twisted and woven to make containers.

The earth itself, when moulded and fired, produced containers. These pottery vessels were fragile and suited more settled societies. 6,000 years ago pottery making was a completely new technology, using the most simple and ancient of materials.

Clay is an easy material to decorate. Using decoration people could quickly ally themselves with particular traditions, or break away. Perhaps some pots carried coded messages. The finest pieces were returned to the earth with the dead.

People designed their pots to fit the function intended - round-bottomed pots to nestle on uneven floors, pots with shoulders to enable covers to be secured, pots for pouring, pots for storing, pots for carrying....[16]

Below left–Someone over 5,000 years ago wove this basket from straw and splinters of wood. It survived in a peat bog in Twyford, Ireland. © National Museum of Ireland, [17] which also owns the object.

Below–Reconstruction of the basket from Twyford. This one is woven from the leaves of the wild iris, Yellow Flag.

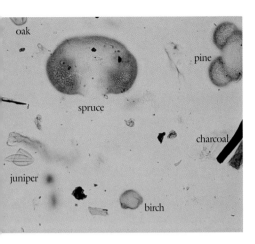

HISTORY IN THE BOG

When vegetation dies it usually leaves no trace. In special cases like when conditions are very wet or very dry, organic material can be preserved. The Moine Mhor or Moss provides perfect waterlogged conditions. This raised bog consists of layers of sphagnum moss and other plants such as sedges which have accumulated over thousands of years to form peat.

In such conditions pollen can be preserved. Deposits containing pollen are retrieved using coring devices, and the pollen grains are isolated in the laboratory and identified under the microscope. The results can be displayed in a pollen diagram, a graphical device which helps us to build a picture of past vegetation and changing environments. No single pollen core from Kilmartin covers the whole 10,000 years since the retreat of the ice. So here we present an amalgamation of information from several sites in the area.[18]

It shows the presence of sedges, grasses and dwarf willows at the end of the last glacial period, all plants which thrive in cold open conditions. As the climate warmed juniper, birch and hazel helped to prepare soil for later arrivals such as oak and elm. The beginning of agriculture is marked by the appearance of cereals and arable weeds, and the decline of the tree pollen suggesting forest clearance.

Some plants produce more pollen than others and this has to be taken into account when using pollen to recreate past environments. Pine produces a lot, while oak produces little. Also, some pollen grains decay more quickly than others. Juniper loses its spherical shape, while rushes disappear altogether from the pollen record. The 7,000 year old material shown here includes charcoal, a valuable indicator of fire.

Barley pollen grain. It is not possible to tell if this grain of barley-type pollen is a wild or cultivated variety. Traces of other parts of the plant such as seeds are needed to complement the evidence from pollen.

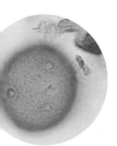

Ribwort plantain. This pollen can be distinguished from other plantains.[19]
It is a plant which likes open ground, and its presence in pollen samples indicates a non-wooded, possibly pastoral landscape.

Pollen diagram bringing together the results of several pollen studies from near Kilmartin.

All graphics Kevin Edwards.

IDEALIZED POLLEN DIAGRAM FOR THE KILMARTIN VALLEY

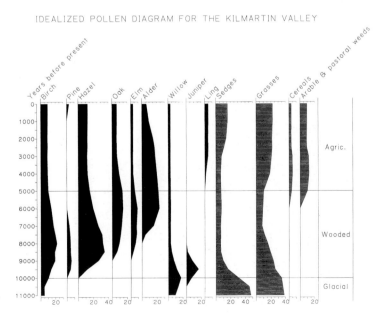

HEAVEN & EARTH

Kilmartin's landscape in about 1,500 BC was dramatic, powerful and awe-inspiring.

A line of at least seven cairns dominated the valley floor.[1] Standing stones–some single, some in complex arrangements - dotted the land-scape, and rock carvings decorated view points and access ways. Precious objects were placed in the cairns in the valley and in stone-built graves on gravel terraces at the valley edges.

These objects and monuments tell us of a sophisticated and wealthy society which had contacts with other parts of Britain, Ireland and the Continent.[2] They provide clues as to how people interacted with their environment, with each other and with their past.

Whatever motivated its evolution, Kilmartin's landscape communicated an overwhelming sense of power - the power of the architects, of the past on which they built, of the universe to which the monuments referred, and of the monuments themselves. This power was both spiritual and political, and its maintenance may have seemed crucial to the continued existence of life in the valley.

Nether Largie standing stones [3] *contributed to the ceremonial nature of the landscape at the time when the linear cemetery was in use, but the stones were probably erected much earlier. The sense of the sacred in the landscape even then was enhanced by the presence of ancient monuments.*

AN ORGANISED LANDSCAPE

Temple Wood.[4] *Kilmartin's ceremonial landscape evolved over a period of at least 2,000 years, culminating in the completion of the linear cemetery around 1,500 BC. People used the site at Temple Wood over the entire period and beyond.*

The monuments which remain in the Kilmartin valley are the remnants of a landscape which bristled with power and meaning.

In the illustration overleaf we have reconstructed the landscape using evidence from many sources: historical archives, aerial photography, archaeological surveys and excavation.

The valley floor is shown free of trees, so that one cairn would be visible from another. The forest, still an important resource, cloaks the hillside with avenues cut for access to the sacred valley. The climate was probably slightly warmer and wetter than it is today, but slowly deteriorating. Future environmental work–for example the analysis of ancient pollen–will help build a clearer picture of the climate and vegetation of the valley in 1,500 BC.

No technique, scientific or archaeological, can yet tell us exactly how the valley was used, but on the evidence of rich artefacts and the disciplined organisation of space, we have envisaged a stratified society with a few important individuals controlling access to and within the valley. People are shown processing in an orderly fashion, echoing the ordered alignment of the most dominant monument, the Linear Cemetery. Some are taking the opportunity to show off their prestigious artefacts.

'The valley is studded with cairns, megaliths, inscribed stones, forts, and other monuments of antiquity. The number of these is but a tithe of what existed two centuries ago: old men alive at the beginning of the last century spoke of more than a score of cairns and many standing stones being removed to make room for the plough or to build dikes and form steadings.' *Gillies 1909.*[5]

Upper Largie [6] looks onto the valley from about the same height as Kilmartin. Excavators found a complex arrangement of pits and several burials, now destroyed by gravel quarrying. A cist, now on display at Kilmartin House, can be seen – dismantled – just below the centre of the photograph. Kilmartin Valley stretches SW into the distance.
Scotia Archaeology Ltd.

KILMARTIN IN 1,500 BC – THE LINEAR CEMET

Kilmartin [7] *(Gaz. 21)*

The church and its former manse – now Kilmartin House – are built on a gravel terrace very similar to the ones at Upper Largie and Bruach an Druimein. Over 3,500 years ago, both were used for rituals relating to the dead. If people had enacted ceremonies here in Kilmartin too, all traces would have disappeared in building the church and village. Here we imagine the sort of monuments that may have existed once - standing stones, earth banks and burial cists.

Missing cairn

Crop marks, seen in aerial photographs, suggest a cairn may have been here.

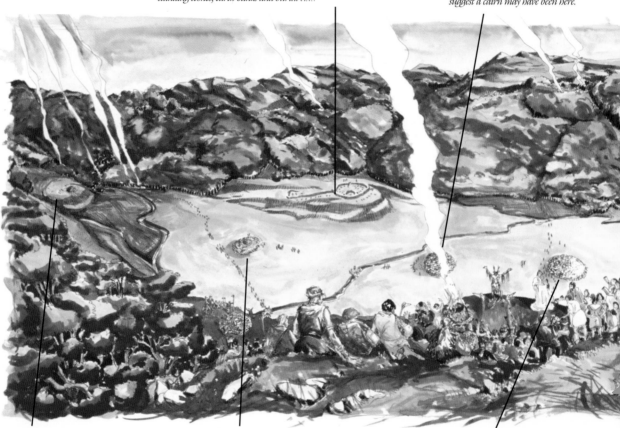

Upper Largie [8]

Much of the remains at Upper Largie have been quarried away. People used the site for burial between about 2,000 - 1,500 BC. It is probable that the site was special even before that: people often place their dead in places which are already important in some way - cairns and cremations near standing stones, graves near churches.

The Glebe cairn [9] *(Gaz. 1)*

Excavators found two small stone circles beneath the cairn with two finely made pots and a jet necklace placed in two cists. The cairn is smaller than it was a century ago - in 1864 it was at least 4 metres high and 33 metres in diameter.

Nether Largie North cairn [10] *(Gaz. 2)*

Removed during excavation in 1930, the cairn's appearance today is a reconstruction. A magnificent capstone was found within the mound, decorated with carvings of bronze flat axes and small hollows or cup marks. There was also a circular earthen bank - perhaps the remains of an even earlier monument.

Nether Largie stones [11] (*Gaz. 7*)

At present five large and eight small stones are visible. A geophysical survey in 1993 suggested that there may have been more stones, and areas enclosed by banks and ditches. This could only be proved by excavation, but here we have suggested what these features may have looked like.

Bruach an Druimein [13]

Nine cists have been found here, but only three are now visible. It was an important place where about 4,000 years ago someone was buried with a precious jet necklace. Traces of settlement have also been found. The site was used in the early Mediaeval period but is otherwise undated. As there is no evidence of settlement elsewhere, we suggest that this might have been where at least some people lived.

Rowanfield & Crinan Moss cists [12]

Now in ruins, these sites are in line with the valley cairns and may once have been cairns too. Grooves have been carved into one of the side slabs, an extremely unusual feature shared with cists in the linear cemetery cairns.

Missing cairn

Various reports suggest that a cairn once existed between Nether Largie Mid and South cairns, though no trace is now visible.

Nether Largie Mid cairn [14] (*Gaz. 3*)

In the 1920s the cairn was three metres high, but by the time it was excavated in 1929 most of the stones had been removed for mending roads and now it is only about a metre high. Two empty cists were found within the mound.

Nether Largie South cairn [15] (*Gaz. 4*)

Containing a stone chamber and built many generations - perhaps 1,000 years - before the other cairns, it may originally have been trapezoidal, not round. It was also used by the makers of the round cairns, who, we suggest here, modified its shape to make it like the others.

Ri Cruin cairn [16] (*Gaz. 5*)

By 1930 very few stones remained, but remnant kerb stones suggest it was about 20 metres in diameter. The cairn has now been reconstructed. One of the cist slabs was decorated with depictions of bronze axe heads, while another was carved with an enigmatic design - possibly a boat or ceremonial weapon.

POWER HOLDERS

We know more about the people who were powerful than those who weren't. One of them wore a magnificent jet necklace and another carried a ceremonial blade or halberd.[17] These were probably the people who dictated how the monuments should be made and used.

Jet for the necklace had to be brought from Yorkshire.[18] A material prized for thousands of years, it is capable of taking a high shine and, like amber, has a magical electrostatic quality. The halberd was made of copper–a substance whose extraction from rock may have been imbued in mystery, secrecy and magic. People in Scotland first used metal objects before 2000 BC but several hundred years later such objects were still rare and special.

Like today, people esteemed similar objects and designs over wide areas. Jet necklaces from Kilmartin, Loch Melfort, Renfrewshire and Angus are all alike.[19] The fine pottery beakers used between 2,500 and 1,500 BC are similar in Kilmartin, Holland and Orkney. While the powerful people of Kilmartin conformed to widespread trends by using such objects, in other ways they were unusual. Carving of grooves on cist slabs is peculiar to Argyll and of 12 grooved cists found in the British Isles, 10 are found in Kilmartin.[20]

Halberd bearer. *The person who held this object commanded a special power. It may not have been an effective weapon, unless for ceremonial fighting, but it was an impressive sign of status. It may have been decked with ribbons or feathers.*

Jet spacer-plate necklace, Kilmartin. *Triangles and lozenges are the commonest motifs on the necklaces, in every case formed by drilling small holes. The specialist skills and tools required to work jet, and the similarity of designs suggest there were relatively few craftspeople making these necklaces, perhaps near the source of the material in Whitby. The photograph shows a reconstruction which, like the original, is made from Whitby jet. The drawings depict components of various necklaces from all over Scotland.*

The original is the property of National Museums of Scotland.

Food vessels, Glebe Cairn. *Of the 17 food vessels found within 6 miles of Kilmartin, 11 are of a type known as Irish Bowls and are very similar to pots found in Ireland. The three-part shape and decorative techniques seen on the pot from the Glebe Cairn, for example, are replicated exactly on pots in Ireland. Many pots found in Kilmartin are exceptionally fine, some with beautifully decorated bases. To show off this decoration the vessel from the Glebe Cairn may have been suspended using the small lugs on its side.* Property of National Museums of Scotland (*upper*) and British Museum (*lower*).

GLEBE CAIRN

Glebe cairn was excavated in 1864 by Canon Greenwell, a churchman from Durham and a leading collector of prehistoric material in Britain. This model, with the cairn itself visible through the window, shows what Greenwell found under the cairn material. [21]

The northernmost cairn in the Linear Cemetery was found to cover stone circles, two cists and rich grave goods. The site may first have consisted of a small enclosure bounded by a double ring of stones. For several hundred years before the construction of the Linear Cemetery, people may have used the circle as a space for meeting, dancing, praying and celebrating.

Later the structure received the remains of Kilmartin's most powerful individuals—people who were buried with fine pottery, possibly imported from Ireland, and a precious jet necklace.

People then covered the cists and the stone circle with a cairn, the monument becoming one of a series of burial monuments in a line, each alike but each hiding a complex history and evoking a glorious past.[22]

The rings of stone under Glebe cairn share some features with the south circle at Temple Wood, a mile away. Similar in size, at both sites three of the standing stones touch and there is evidence for dry stone walling. Neither can be dated accurately, but the south circle at Temple Wood may date to around 3,000 BC. [23]

BUILDING ON THE PAST

Four thousand years ago people reused nearly all of Kilmartin's earlier monuments.

The stone circle at Temple Wood and the circular enclosure of Ballymeanoch henge had been special places in the landscape for many generations. Hundreds of years after their construction, people placed burial cists in both monuments. They placed their dead in places which were already recognized for their antiquity and spiritual power.

Similarly the linear cemetery was built on old foundations. When people built round cairns on top of the older structures, and added others–all in a line–they unified the landscape. The space between became as important as the monuments themselves. The valley was now dominated by one composite monument, and the whole landscape expressed the power and importance of its architects.

We do not know if the older monuments represented a power to be drawn upon or neutralised. They clearly could not be ignored, and played an important part in defining each new generation's own power and identity.

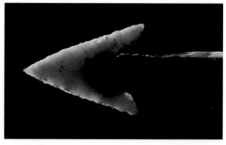

Reconstructed arrow. *Two of the burials inserted into earlier monuments were accompanied by arrows. Perhaps they were signs of aggression, or were they simply symbols of their owner's prowess in hunting?*

Ballymeanoch Henge. *Henges are circular areas bounded by a ditch and bank, built between about 3,200 and 2,200 BC. They are only found in the British Isles. The one shown here is the only one known in western Scotland.* [24]

Nether Largie South was built about 3,000 BC. It housed the remains of many people, and was probably in use over many generations. It was where the living and the dead met, a place where the dead ancestors of the community could be invoked to bring strength and prosperity. Not everyone could be placed in the tomb, but it was probably a monument with which the whole community could identify. [25]

Beakers from Nether Largie South (left), and Ballymeanoch henge (right) and a replica Beaker from Temple Wood (centre). Flint arrow from Nether Largie South. *People made Beakers throughout France, Germany, Holland, England and Scotland from about 2,500 to 1,500 BC. 13 were found in Kilmartin – some inserted into older monuments, others in isolated cists. The Beakers shown here were all deposited in places in the landscape which were already sacred. Both Ballymeanoch henge and Nether Largie South chambered cairn were many generations old when people inserted the burial cists and Beakers. The Beaker at Temple Wood was not placed directly inside the ancient circle, but in a cist on the perimeter. With the Beaker burials both there and at Nether Largie South people placed several arrows. Perhaps these vessels once were filled with intoxicating substances – either for the mourners, or perhaps for the dead. A Beaker in Fife contained traces of mead.* Original Beakers and arrowhead property of British Museum.

CARVED ROCKS

Carved rock surface, Ormaig. [26]
Carvings often occupy prominent places in the landscape such as route-ways and places with a good view.

Rock carvings have a more subtle impact than cairns and standing stones, but they undoubtedly affected the way people felt as they moved through the landscape. They are found on bedrock, boulders, cists, standing stones and in cairns.

The concentration of carvings in Mid Argyll is exceptional; there are over 100 sites within six miles of Kilmartin, while Kintyre has 12 and Lorn only one.[27] Cup and ring marks are by far the most common type in Mid Argyll. Similar concentrations occur in Dumfries, Galloway and Northumbria.[28]

Precise dating of the carvings is difficult because the simple motifs –cup marks in particular–have been used over a huge time span–from at least 4,000 BC in Scotland.[29] Carvings found in the Linear Cemetery and in associated cist cemeteries cannot have been done later than about 1,500 BC, but they might have been carved long before this.

The most enigmatic design is carved in a cist under the cairn at Ri Cruin. It appears to represent something real, but we can't work out what.

Hundreds of suggestions have been made as to the purpose of cup and ring marks, such as:

- ✕ meeting places
- ✕ places for initiation rites
- ✕ marking territories
- ✕ mapping stars
- ✕ maps
- ✕ aids for copper prospecting
- ✕ musical instruments
- ✕ platforms for exposing the dead
- ✕ boundary markers
- ✕ graffiti
- ✕ secret language
- ✕ decoration
- ✕ religious symbols

Carving from Ri Cruin cairn. *It could be a boat, or could it be a halberd decorated with ribbons?* [30]

64

HAVING THE EDGE

Bronze blade, Loch Glashan. *Axes are rarely found in graves, but daggers and blades are relatively common. Shown here beside the original from Loch Glashan is a reconstruction of how the blade might have looked when new.*

Upper photo © Trustees of National Museums of Scotland. Object owned by NMS.

◄ Horned spiral from Achnabreck. *Attempts have been made to date some carvings by comparing them with similar designs elsewhere. This spiral, a spiral at Temple Wood, stars and plain rings, for example, may relate to Irish passage art from about 3,000 BC.*[31]

◄ Cist slab from Badden, near Lochgilphead, *decorated with an unusual design similar to Irish carvings 5,000 years old. The grooves on the slab cut through the design, suggesting it was originally made for another purpose. Grooves on another cist slab from Kilmartin were similarly cut across a cup mark.* Property of Glasgow Museums: Art Gallery and Museum Kelvingrove.[32]

The first metalworkers may have seemed like magicians. The act of changing stone into liquid and then into a shining, sharp edged tool represented a new level of manipulation of the natural world.

Metalworking required a greater degree of specialisation than making pottery or working stone, and sufficient organisation to bring together raw materials. The nearest source of tin–a key component of bronze–was Cornwall.

The first copper objects in Europe date from about 4,000 BC and there is evidence for metalworking in Ireland by at least 2,500 BC. The first copper objects in Scotland are the copper knives which often accompanied burials containing beakers. Such knives are reported from cists near Kilmartin, but they have not survived.[33]

Carved axes, Ri Cruin cairn. *Although few copper or bronze objects have survived from Kilmartin the importance of the new technology is suggested by the unique carvings of bronze flat axes in three of the Linear Cemetery cairns.*[34]

Flat axe moulds, *NE Scotland. The earliest metal objects were made in stone moulds. No such moulds have been found in Argyll, nor is there evidence for copper working. Copper mines lie less than a mile from Kilmartin, but nineteenth century working has destroyed any evidence of prehistoric workings that might have existed. The oldest carbon dated copper mines in NW Europe are in Cork, Ireland.* Society of Antiquaries of Scotland.[35]

ALIGNMENT

Within a six mile radius of Kilmartin there are 25 sites with standing stones. 13 are single stones, 11 are arrangements and one–Temple Wood–consists of two circles.

The stones show little uniformity in appearance–from small to very tall, from smooth to angular, from plain to decorated. Group arrangements vary from a cross shape at Nether Largie to two parallel lines at Ballymeanoch. Both have stones outside the arrangement known as outliers. Some single stones may originally have been part of a group, and some sites have disappeared altogether.

Standing stones are difficult to date. A deposit in a stone hole at Temple Wood was 5,000 years old, but some stones might be quite modern. Carvings on stones at Nether Largie and Ballymeanoch suggest they were erected at least 3,500 years ago. [36]

Two hundred years ago the stones near Kilmartin were thought to commemorate people who had fallen in land conflicts. More recently it has been suggested that the stones were meticulously aligned to chart the movement of the sun, moon and stars for the calculation of a calendar - that they are the earliest evidence in Argyll of people's desire to fix themselves precisely in time. [37]

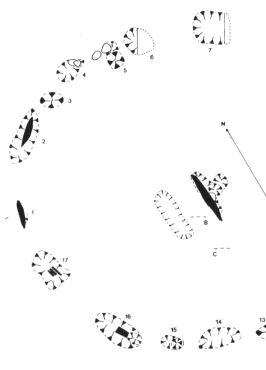

Temple Wood *excavations revealed a circle to the north of the stones now visible. The central pit, plus pits marked 3, 5, 12 and 13 on this plan, may represent the remains of an observatory set up to predict the midwinter solstice.* Jack Scott. [39]

There was a total eclipse of the sun *at Kilmartin at 11.25 am on 29th July 1629 BC. Would our ancestors have wanted to predict such an event, and if so, would they have had the ability?* [38]

Brainport Bay monument *points towards the mid-summer sunrise. It is suggested that the mid-winter sunset and the equinoxes could also be observed from here.* [40] Col. Peter Fane Gladwin.

Stones at Nether Largie *illustrate some of the difficulties in alignment theories. Alignments have been deduced with the midwinter sunrise, sunrise on the winter quarter days, the full moon's major northern standstill and moonrise at the minor standstills. But with such an arrangement of stones, alignment with at least one celestial event is almost inevitable, and precise intentions remain difficult to prove.* [41]

ORIENTATION

Even where exact alignment cannot be shown, many monuments– not just standing stones–are deliberately orientated in particular directions.

The entrance to Nether Largie South chambered cairn is at the north-east, and this is the same for nearly all cairns of this type. Passage tombs in Ireland, on the other hand, are entered from the south-east, and the circles in Aberdeen have their one horizontal slab consistently to the south-west. Even today, many churches have an east-west orientation.

These sites look outward to the skies, and beyond to death, for nearly all were primarily or secondarily for the disposal and celebration of the dead. By orientating monuments in particular ways the passage from life to death was perhaps linked symbolically to the movement of the sun, moon and stars.

Monuments in the landscape were designed to take on special qualities at specific times of the day, month or year–to be lit by the sun in a particular way at dawn or at midwinter, for example. Thus they linked the land, the cycles of nature and the poles of life and death, helping to orientate people in time and place.

Kintraw Sunset

Standing stone and cairn, Kintraw. [42]

It has been argued that the position of the cairn and stone at Kintraw would enable people to make precise observations of the midwinter sunset, but there are other features at the site whose positioning seems more symbolic than scientific. The blocked entrance or false portal (right) seems more for the dead than the living. Its orientation towards the south-south west - the extreme southern moonset - may have been important for religious or traditional reasons.

D Simpson. *(plan and black and white photo of Kintraw)*

Reproduced courtesy of the Society of Antiquaries of Scotland.

STANDING S

CAIRN B

CIST

Kintraw Portal Stone

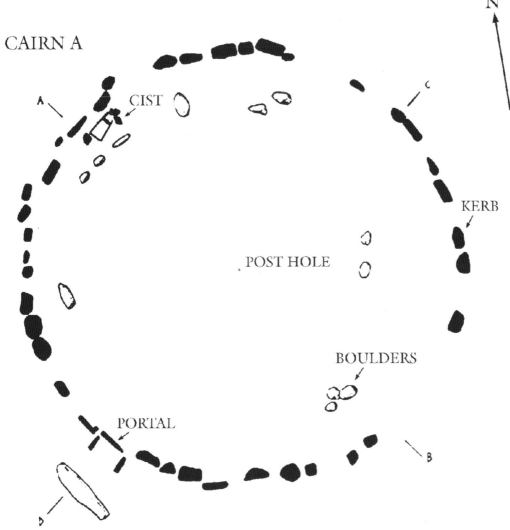

CAIRN A

N

A

CIST

C

KERB

POST HOLE

BOULDERS

PORTAL

B

BOGS & METALWORK

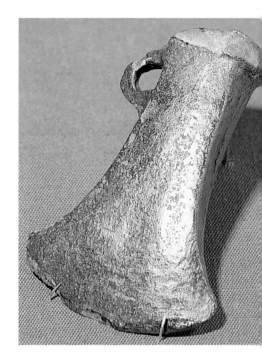

In about 700 BC someone thrust three swords into a bog on an island 7 miles from Kilmartin. At around the same time someone left a collection of metal objects on the banks of Loch Awe at Torran, near Ford. [43]

No trace of these people survives–no habitation, burial mound or megalith. Things were very different from a thousand years earlier, when the Linear Cemetery was constructed.

It was a time of continuing poor climate–cold and wet. The area of marshy land and blanket peat was increasing and there was less good farming land.[44] The landscape now provided another challenge.

Socketed axe, Poltalloch. *Found with a spearhead at an unspecified location near Kilmartin, this axe, from about 700–800 BC, is about the same date as the Glashan axe and the two hoards.*
Property of National Museums of Scotland.

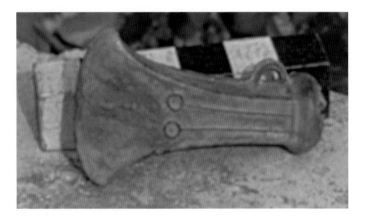

Socketed axe, Loch Glashan. *Found by a 14 year old boy in a loch near Kilmartin, this is one of the very few bronze axes which is decorated.*
Marion Campbell.
Property of National Museums of Scotland.

Depositing the Shuna swords. *The artist imagines three powerful people stabbing the swords into the bog while other members of the community look on.*

Kerb cairn in front of Ballymeanoch stones. *One of the few monuments which survives from the period between the flourishing of the linear cemetery and the time when the swords were deposited on the island of Shuna. With other kerb cairns at Kintraw and Temple Wood, it probably dates to about 1300 BC.*[45]

Mòine Mhór or Moss.

It is not clear exactly when the peat began to form on the Crinan Moss. Whenever it was, the hostility of the resultant landscape to human occupation must have had a profound effect on where and how people lived.[46]

OBJECTS IN THE LANDSCAPE

The Shuna swords, found pointing downwards in a bog, contrast with the assortment of bronze axes, rings and spearheads found on a dry bank at Torran. It was probably for different reasons that people left these valuable objects behind.

The three swords, like a ring of six shields left in a bog in Ayrshire, look as if people placed them in the bog deliberately, perhaps during some kind of ceremony. Prehistoric metalwork is often found in wet places. Perhaps the waters were the medium by which gifts could be sacrificed to gods or to the spirits of the place.[47]

The objects found at Torran do not look like a ceremonial offering. They vary in quality. One of the axes is badly pitted, another was badly cast, but a third is pristine. Perhaps they were the stock of a smith. But somehow, for reasons we can only imagine, these objects–stashed in haste or with care–were never recovered.

The artist envisages a procession of horn players and other members of this accomplished society. Perhaps some of the horns are to be broken–'killed'–and thrown onto the bog.

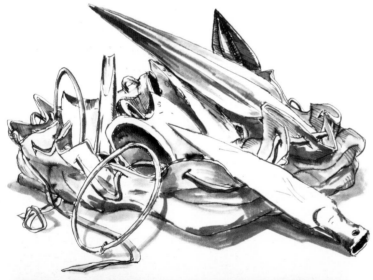

The Torran Hoard was described as slightly sticky when found. Perhaps it was originally in a leather bag.

The Torran Hoard,[48] *soon after discovery. The objects were found in two phases. Some of them were found by a boy digging out a ferret in 1881. The remainder were found by Marion Campbell and Mary Sandeman in 1962 when they were making an inventory of archaeological sites in Mid Argyll. They were led to the site by the late Alistair Carmichael who remembered being shown the spot as a boy by the original finder, then an old man. Marion Campbell.* Property of National Museums of Scotland.

MUSIC & METALWORK

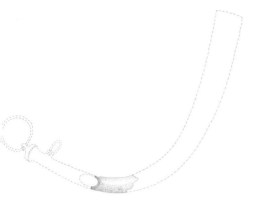

Fragment of bronze horn, Wigtownshire, *showing how it may have fitted into the whole. Although this is the only horn found so far in Scotland it is likely that people here were familiar with the sound of the horn. Over 100 horns have been found in Ireland, a country whose ancient links with Argyll are well established.* [49] Anne Taylor
Fragment property of National Museums of Scotland.

Seascape with the island of Shuna.

It is likely that music was an important ingredient of prehistoric life, as it is today. But most instruments were made of perishable materials like wood or skin, or are too simple for us to recognise such as rhythm sticks and stone drums.

The bronze Irish Horn is an exception. Through it we hear the voice of prehistory. It tells us of people who were wealthy, technically accomplished and well organised.

The skill of these people was such that even today's most accomplished metalworker cannot create such a fine light instrument. They were rich enough to sacrifice up to 50 horns in bogs.[50]

We do not know what created their wealth. Perhaps it was the cattle, whose horns the instruments resemble, and whose voice the horn can mimic. Cattle are central to much of Irish legend,[51] perhaps with its roots in this period. Kilmartin itself was celebrated for the quality of its cattle until very recent times:

'Even the highest hills are covered with a deep rich friable soil, affording fine herbage for the cattle and sheep, for which this district is so celebrated.' *Second Statistical Account, 1845.*

FRIENDS & ENEMIES

By the first centuries AD people lived in a completely new kind of landscape.

They no longer used cairns on the valley floor to bury their dead and the standing stones had lost the meaning they had held thousands of years before. Less physical effort was spent on honouring dead ancestors and more on protecting those still living.

New sorts of buildings dominated the landscape–monuments which seem to reflect insecurity and distrust. Strongly walled dwellings crowned the hilltops, and in the lochs people built artificial islands to live on. Access ways on land, loch and coast were overshadowed by these powerful buildings. This would have affected the way people felt when moving through the landscape.

This section focuses on the landscape of the 6–8th centuries AD, a time when the fort of Dunadd was flourishing and the island dwelling on Loch Glashan was occupied. Many of the hilltop sites were constructed earlier, and some may have fallen out of use, but they still would have affected the way people viewed Kilmartin's landscape.

This was the time when monks were bringing a new religion to Scotland from Ireland–an ideology which would profoundly influence social structure and how people perceived their landscape, their rulers and themselves.

The hillfort of Dunadd *protruding from the Mòine Mhór*

SURVIVING ON A LOCH

From at least 300 BC, some people in Argyll chose to live in lochs on artificial islands known as crannogs. The evidence showing how people lived on these is well preserved; wood and leather can survive in water for thousands of years.

Of the hundreds of tons of material which excavating a crannog can produce, only a selection can be preserved. Apart from everyday objects and samples showing clear tool marks, even quite plain pieces of wood can throw light on aspects of life in the past. The diameter, straightness and lack of knots on wood, for example, can imply woodland management with techniques such as coppicing and pollarding.

Excavation is only one technique employed by underwater archaeologists. Sites can be discovered and plans, sometimes very detailed, produced through non-destructive surveys: aerial photography, ultrasonic soundings of the loch bottom and side-scan sonar. [1]

Two fragments of polished burr wood –*possibly blackthorn–were found on Loch Glashan crannog. Perhaps people used them as gaming pieces.*
Property of Glasgow Museums:
Art Gallery and Museum Kelvingrove.

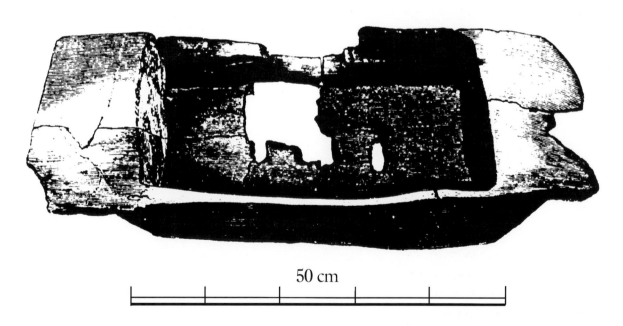

50 cm

On exposure to air organic objects require special treatment. This trough from Lochlee, Ayrshire was complete when found in 1882, but 'upon drying, quickly crumbled into dust'. This drawing is all that now remains. [2]

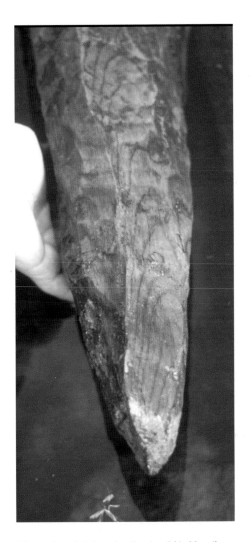

Microscopic analysis shows that the point of this alder pile from Oakbank crannog on Loch Tay *was carved with an iron axe. This 2,500 year old object could be preserved either by keeping it wet, or by chemical treatment.* Scottish Underwater Archaeological Trust.

Reverend Mapleton, Episcopalian Dean of Argyll, was one of the first people to use underwater investigation in archaeology. Here the artist reconstructs Mapleton's exploration of the crannog in Loch Coille-Bharr *in 1870, for which he borrowed divers employed on the Crinan Canal.* [3]

ISLAND LANDSCAPE

Twenty crannogs have been found on Loch Awe and there are probably more.[4] Some of them are visible as small piles of stones up to 50
metres from the shore. Many are only visible from the air or when
the water level is very low.

Radiocarbon dating tells us that people lived on one of the
crannogs near Ford around 300 BC. Evidence from elsewhere shows
that crannogs were in use from 1,500 BC - 1,700 AD, so the Loch
Awe crannogs could cover a long period of time.[5]

In recent times crannogs have been considered as places of
defence and refuge. However, their construction required organisation, vision and domination of the local environment making it likely that some were also symbols of status and power. They may also
have provided security for animals, goods or agricultural produce.

Whatever their purpose a cluster of crannogs would have a significant effect on the landscape. The construction of five crannogs
would have required several acres of woodland to be cleared and
once built they would have a commanding appearance. Even if only
a quarter of the crannogs on Loch Awe were occupied at any one
time land and water access would be affected, as well as the peace we
now imagine to be characteristic of Scottish lochs.

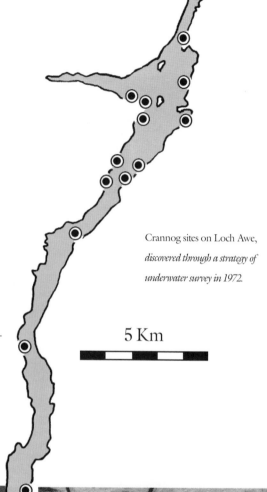

Crannog sites on Loch Awe,
discovered through a strategy of
underwater survey in 1972.

5 Km

Crannog, Loch Awe.

Blaeu's 17th century map of Scotland *shows many island*
dwellings, indicated with the icon shown here, and sometimes
labelled 'crannokis'.

ISLAND LODGE

French wheel-turned pottery is found at Loch Glashan and Dunadd and it is possible that the same people, perhaps relatives, lived in the two places.

Bronze brooch, typical of the 8th century AD found on Loch Glashan crannog. It is made with amber which probably came from the Baltic.

One of the few crannogs to have been excavated is on Loch Glashan, seven miles south east of Kilmartin. It was revealed when the water level was reduced for a hydro-electric scheme. Its remains now lie a few metres below the surface. [6]

1200 years ago the crannog was a high status site where fine jewellery was worn, and which received prestigious imported goods from France. There were craftsmen on the crannog working metal and making leather goods.[7]

People lived in Loch Glashan crannog when Argyll was occupied by Gaelic speaking people from Ireland who had settled around Kilmartin in the 6th century AD. One of their main centres was Dunadd hill fort, six miles from Loch Glashan.

Dunadd and the Loch Glashan crannog have different characters. Dunadd's carvings, architecture and the quantity of exotic goods found there suggest it was a trade centre, a place for ritual and for royal hospitality. Although a prestigious site, the function of the Loch Glashan crannog may have been more practical.

Numerous fragments of leather were found including offcuts, suggesting that leather items were manufactured here.

All three artefacts are the property of Glasgow Museums: Art Gallery and Museum Kelvingrove.

During excavations at Loch Glashan in 1970 a log boat was found beside the crannog.
Marion Campbell.
Property of Glasgow Museums: Art Gallery and Museum Kelvingrove.

A TENSE LANDSCAPE

For more than 1,000 years from about 500 BC people built fortified structures. Of the 30 of these which crown the hills surrounding Kilmartin, few have been securely dated, and so we cannot say how many would have been occupied at one time. [8]

Even if only a quarter were in use simultaneously, the character of the landscape would have been severe, with access points not decorated with rock carvings as they had been several thousand years before, but dominated by hill forts. The landscape was now not known by reference to gods and ancestors but by reference to living political leaders and petty tyrants.

By 700 AD when people were living in the fort at Dunadd and on the Loch Glashan crannog, many of the hilltop sites would have been ancient ruins. Some, however, such as the sophisticated double-walled structure at Ardifuar, were still occupied and probably had links with Dunadd which was the focal site of the area.

One object was carried through the generations, linking pre-history with history: the carved stone ball found with 7th–8th century AD material at Dunadd was by then already 2,500 years old.

The 8th century inhabitants of Ardifuar used a site that was already ancient, possibly built 700 years earlier. How did they feel about the other even older monuments around Kilmartin? Some sites may have been covered by peat, but others such as the standing stones at Ballymeanoch and Temple Wood would have still been visible. They will have had stories to tell of these ancient places.

Ardifuar [10]

Objects such as a crucible and imported pottery show that Ardifuar was used in the 6-8th century AD, but the architecture suggests that the structure was built in the 1-2nd century AD.

Duntroon [11]

Thirty-six saddle querns were found at Duntroon fort. By the 1st century BC most people used the more efficient rotary quern.

Castle Dounie [9] with Ardifuar in the background. *Sightings from here could perhaps have been communicated to Dunadd, where visibility is more restricted.*

Eilean Righ [12]

The knife and glass bead from here date to around the 8th century AD.

Dùn Chonallaich [13]

The stone gaming board found here is of early historic date.

Dùn na Nighinn [14]

Dunadd [15]

Most finds from Dunadd date to the 6-8th centuries AD, but a few objects - a ring headed pin, some finger rings and Roman pottery - are earlier.

Druim an Duin [16]

The portion of rotary quern found here shows the site was used after the 1st century BC.

DUNADD

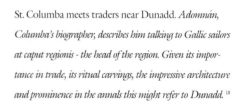

Rising out of the flat expanse of the Moine Mhor, Dunadd stands sentinel as the River Add snakes around its feet. Sections of wall and some enigmatic rock carvings tell of a time over a thousand years ago, when Dunadd was an imposing and strongly defended fort.

Excavation tells us that from 500–1,000 AD, Dunadd was an important centre for trade with the continent. Its people were in contact with monks on Iona and the aristocracy of Northumbria, and it was a place where skilled metal-workers crafted jewellery and tools in bronze, silver and gold.

To archaeology is added the first written evidence, and for the first time we can put names to the people inhabiting Argyll– Fergus, Oengus, Loarn. These Celtic-speaking members of the Irish aristocracy came to Argyll in the early 6th century AD.[17] Both they and the people of Ireland were at that time known as Scotti, and it is from them that Scotland later took its name.

St. Columba meets traders near Dunadd. *Adomnán, Columba's biographer, describes him talking to Gallic sailors at caput regionis - the head of the region. Given its importance in trade, its ritual carvings, the impressive architecture and prominence in the annals this might refer to Dunadd.* [18]

Metalworking. *The craftsman is shown in the sort of lean-to represented by post holes at Dunadd. Extremely sophisticated techniques were undertaken - gold and silver casting, filigree, interlace and glass settings.* [19]

Crucible and brooch mould (left), mould of bird-headed brooch (centre), reconstruction of bird-headed brooch (right), all from Dunadd. *Fragments of 50 brooch moulds and 263 crucibles were found at Dunadd. This brooch is a reconstruction based on one of the 7 moulds for bird-headed brooches. Microscopic analysis showed that the crucible shown here had been used for gold.*
Original artefacts, National Museums of Scotland.

KINGS & SAINTS

Incised slate, Dunadd. *The form of writing on this slate suggests a date of about 700 AD.*
© Trustees of the National Museums of Scotland. Object owned by NMS.

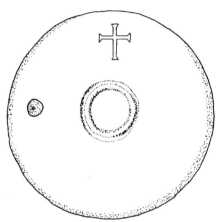

Quern (grinding) stone inscribed with a cross, from Dunadd.[25] *Of at least 20 querns from Dunadd only this and one other were not of local stone. The cross is similar to crosses found on Iona and at other sites in Argyll connected with St Columba.* Ewan Campbell.
Property of National Museums of Scotland.

Carved into the bedrock high on Dunadd's crags are some of Scotland's most intriguing carvings–a footprint and a basin. In the 15th century the Lords of the Isles on Islay used such symbols when power was being passed from one ruler to the next.[20] It may be that by then the tradition was already ancient.

Adomnán's description in 690 AD of the investiture of King Áedán by St. Columba in 574 AD is the first record of an event like this occurring in Europe.[21] Both parties benefited from such an association–Áedán by the spiritual confirmation of his worldly power, and St Columba by becoming a king maker.

The links between Christianity and royalty are represented in the charismatic character of Columba himself who was of the same aristocratic Irish blood as the king he crowned.[22] He could himself have been a king, but instead chose to establish the monastery of Iona. He combined the power and authority of a royal warrior with the devotion and wisdom of a monk.

Dunadd itself fuses memories of political struggle and religious endeavour. Its architecture is aggressive and swords and spears were found there. But also found were a quern stone inscribed with a cross and a carving of the beginning of a phrase in Latin meaning 'In the name of our Father'.

I beg that me, a little man
trembling and most wretched,
rowing through the infinite storm of this age,
Christ may draw after Him to the lofty
most beautiful haven of life
...an unending
holy hymn forever.

Written in the 6th or 7th century, possibly by St. Columba. [23]

A king is inaugurated at Dunadd in the 7th century A.D. [24]

WRITING

The first written inscriptions in Kilmartin commemorate people with Irish names–Finn and Crónán. Irish is the first language we know people spoke in Kilmartin. Before that people may have spoken another branch of the Celtic tongue–p Celtic–more similar to Welsh. Earlier still we don't know what words people used.[26]

The first literate people were Christians, often monks. They frequently wrote in Latin, a language which was internationally understood. They read and copied works from the far east, from Italy and from France.[27] This new level of communication gave the church extra authority and mystique. It also meant that the monks had a hand in our understanding of the history of that time, because they wrote it down. The earliest annals which relate to Kilmartin–the 683 and 736 AD entries about Dunadd–were both recorded by monks on Iona.[28]

This poem, in Latin, may date from the 6th century. From treating and preparing calf hide to its decoration with imported pigments, the copying of scripture was an important monastic function. It is probable that monks produced manuscripts at Cella Diuni, an unlocated Columban foundation on Loch Awe, possibly at Annat.[32]

Likewise, it is the Scots who tell the story of the union of the Picts and Scots in 842 AD under Kenneth MacAlpin.[29] Lacking the other side of the story we will never fully know what happened. In entering the realm of history in Kilmartin it is soon apparent that the written word has equal and opposite powers–to enlighten and to distort.

Stone inscribed with ogham script, Poltalloch [30](replica). The writing carved on this stone was first used in Ireland in the 5th century AD. Many such inscriptions, mostly commemorating individuals, have survived. Three have been found in Argyll - on the island of Gigha, at Dunadd, and this one. It reads CRÓNÁN, a common Irish name of the 9th century AD. Original stone property of National Museums of Scotland.

Cross from Barnakill[31] The inscription on this cross, found just one mile from Dunadd, has been interpreted in various ways including XRI REITON, meaning In the name of Christ, Reiton. It probably dates to the 7th - 8th century AD.

Early Christian cross on Eileach an Naoimh, Garvellachs–
known as Eithne's grave. [33]

Decorated slab carved with crosses on both sides, Achadh na
Cille, Oib. [34] Property of Glasgow Museums:
Art Gallery and Museum Kelvingrove.

In the landscape surrounding Kilmartin people still live, love, dance, mourn, farm, hunt, play and pray. We continue to use the landscape and it continues to affect us in many ways.

We now have the power to make changes more quickly and on a grander scale than ever before. But we can also make informed choices about whether to make these changes or not. There is growing support for the treatment of the landscape as a whole, ensuring a balance is found between its economic, cultural, ecological, educational and æsthetic values. This can best be achieved through increased understanding of the landscape itself among the widest range of people.

This museum guide, based on the displays at Kilmartin House, has looked at some of the contrasting ways people have used Kilmartin's landscape over the past 10,000 years. We hope you enjoy exploring this special place where footprints of the past are all around.

Kilmartin House Museum

Glebe Cairn

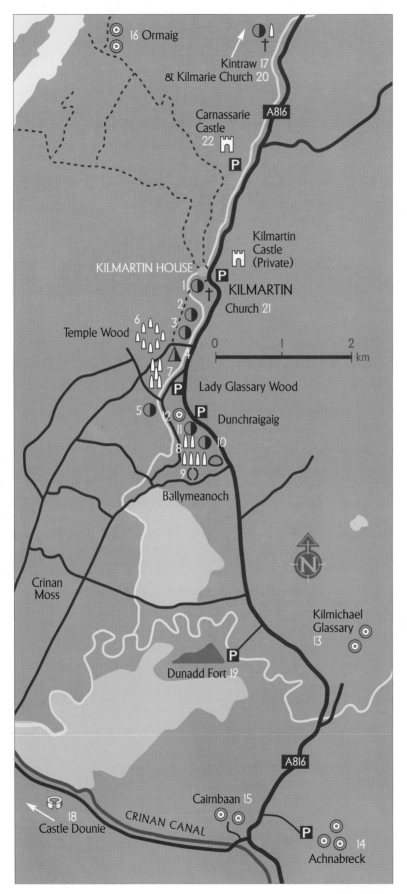

Map of Kilmartin Valley showing sites described in gazetteer

16 Ormaig

Kintraw 17
& Kilmarie Church 20

Carnassarie
Castle
22

A816

Kilmartin
Castle
(Private)

KILMARTIN HOUSE

KILMARTIN

Church 21

1

2

6
3
Temple Wood
4
7

Lady Glassary Wood

5   12

Dunchraigaig
11
8   10
9

Ballymeanoch

Crinan
Moss

Kilmichael
Glassary
13

Dunadd Fort 19

Cairnbaan 15

CRINAN CANAL

Castle Dounie 18

Achnabreck

14

● *Round Cairn*

▲ *Chambered Cairn*

◊ *Standing Stones*

◉ *Fort/Dun*

⌂ *Castle*

◎ *Rock Carving*

† *Christian Site*

⬬ *Barrow*

() *Henge*

0   1   2
km

Access

Ownership of sites is stated in individual entries. Most are in the care of Historic Scotland on behalf of the Secretary of State for Scotland. Please park only in the designated areas, and do not take vehicles onto private roads.

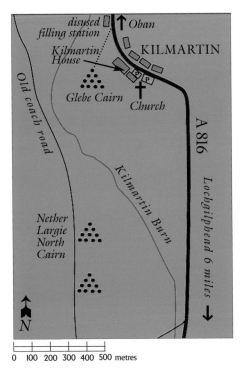

Nether Largie North cairn with Kilmartin behind

1. Glebe Cairn *NR 833 989*

The rounded pile of stones in the field behind the Museum is a burial cairn dating to between 2000 and 1500 BC. It is the most northerly of Kilmartin's linear cemetery–a line of 5 cairns stretching for over a mile along the valley floor.

Excavations were conducted in 1864 by Rev. Greenwell, a Canon from Durham Cathedral. Under the cairn he found two rings of stones and two burial cists. One cist contained a fine pottery vessel with an intricately decorated base (see p 61 & cover) and a jet necklace (see p 60). Both this pot, and the one from the other cist, are similar in shape and decoration to pottery found in Ireland (see p 61). The latter pot, which is owned by the British Museum, can be seen at Kilmartin House. The other alternates between the Museum of Scotland and Kilmartin House. The jet necklace was destroyed by fire at Poltalloch House, formerly the primary residence of the local laird (see p 26).

Access

Cars should be left in Kilmartin. Access is through a gate beside a former filling station on the A816 about 200m north of Kilmartin House. Alternative access is planned, to link the Glebe cairn with the others in the linear cemetery (see below). The Glebe Cairn is in the care of Historic Scotland.

2. Nether Largie North *NR 830 984*

This cairn is another of the burial cairns in Kilmartin's linear cemetery (see nos. 1, 3, 4, 5).

It was excavated in 1930 by Joseph Craw who found a low bank surrounding a large central cist. The cist's cover was decorated with carved axeheads and cupmarks, but all that remained inside was charcoal, ochre and a human tooth. The cairn has recently been rebuilt; you can enter it from the top and see the decorated cist slab inside.

Under the cairn material Craw also found a pointed slab carved with circles (see p 4). The cairn itself probably dates to around 2000 –1500 BC, but the slab could be earlier. This slab is on loan to Kilmartin House Museum from the National Museums of Scotland.

Access to sites no 2–7

The linear cemetery, Temple Wood and Nether Largie stones can all be accessed from Lady Glassary Wood car park, one mile south of Kilmartin.

There is parking in two places **strictly** for people with disabilities: immediately beside the Temple Wood stone circles and about 50m from Ri Cruin cairn.

These sites are in the care of Historic Scotland with the exception of the Nether Largie stones (no. 7) where a management agreement between Historic Scotland and the landowner is currently in place, which enables free public access.

Nether Largie Mid Cairn

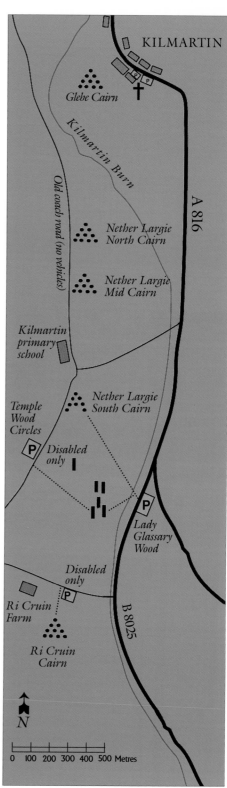

3. Nether Largie Mid Cairn *NR 830 983*

This is the middle cairn of the five burial cairns making up Kilmartin's linear cemetery (see nos. 1,2,4,5). When excavated in 1929 Joseph Craw found 2 cists. Neither contained artefacts, but one was decorated with carvings of axeheads and the other was grooved so that the end slabs could be neatly inserted into the side slabs. The axe-marked cist is still visible but the other is now indicated by concrete posts. (Access–see no. 2)

4. Nether Largie South *NR 828 979*

Nether Largie South is the only chambered cairn of Kilmartin's linear cemetery (see also nos. 1,2,3,5). While the other cairns consist of cists covered by stones, Nether Largie South is more substantial with stone chambers carefully built to receive the bones of the dead over several generations. It is older than the other cairns, probably dating to about 3,000 BC, but it was also used later for burials in cists.

The cairn was excavated in 1864 when Canon Greenwell found evidence for several different burial practices. You can see a decorated round-bottomed pot from the cairn in Kilmartin House museum. People placed this pot in the cairn with remains of their dead probably over 4,500 years ago. Another pot– a Beaker (p 63)–can also be seen in the museum. The Beaker and some arrows were put in the cairn several hundred years after the cairn was built.

(Access–see no. 2)

Nether Largie South chambered cairn

Ri Cruin cairn

Temple Wood southern circle

Temple Wood southern circle

5. Ri Cruin cairn *NR 825 971*

The cairn at Ri Cruin is the most southerly survivor of Kilmartin's linear cemetery (see nos. 1-4). It dates to about 2,000–1500 BC.

The cairn has been excavated three times and its present appearance is largely a reconstruction. Three cists were found. The only contents were some cremated bone in one cist, and in another a stone slab decorated with an unusual carving–thought by some to represent a boat and by others a ceremonial weapon (see p 64). The slab was destroyed in a fire but a cast can be seen in the National Museums of Scotland.

Some carvings which you can still see on site are the axehead carvings on one of the cist slabs (see p 65). They are similar to those at Nether Largie North cairn. (Access–see no. 2)

6. Temple Wood circles *NR 826 978*

This site was used for over 2,000 years from about 3,500 BC. The northern setting in wood was erected first, possibly initially as a solar observatory. The northern structure was later replaced, at least partially, by a circle of stones. People started to build another circle to the south in about 3,000 BC. Burials in cists were added several hundred years later. A replica of the fine pottery Beaker found in one of the two cists can be seen in Kilmartin House Museum (see p 63). The original, accompanied by the flint arrowheads with which it was found, is in St Mungo's Museum of Religious Life in Glasgow.

Carbon dates from a cist in the centre of the circle show that the site was still in use about 1400 BC. Later still the circle was used as a convenient hiding place for some 9th century coins. These were uncovered in the early 19th century when peat was being removed from the valley to make way for improved agricultural practices (see p 22).

This is one of the few sites in the valley which has been excavated thoroughly using modern excavation techniques. (Access–see no. 2)

7. Nether Largie stones *NR 828 976*

This stone setting, 250m SE of Temple Wood stone circles, comprises two pairs of uprights with settings of four and five stones in between. Two out-lying stones survive. Three stones are decorated with carvings.

Examination in conjunction with Temple Wood stone circles (no. 6) has persuaded some commentators that the complex was used in the early second millennium BC as a lunar observatory. It is not, however, known if the sites are contemporaneous. Recent geophysical survey suggests that other features and earthworks may have been associated with the settings.

(Access–see no.2)

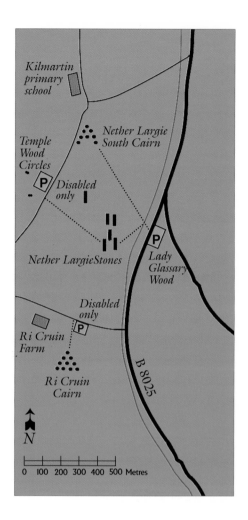

Nether Largie Stones

8. Ballymeanoch stones *NR 833 964*

Of at least 7 standing stones only 6 remain in situ. They are grouped in two parallel lines, each running south east–north west. One line consists of 4 stones, 2 of which are decorated with cup marks and cup-and-ring marks. The 2 stones of the other line are undecorated. A seventh stone used to stand W N W of the two undecorated stones. Cremated bone was found under the stump and the remains of the stone itself can be found dumped in a drain to the east of the stones, near a small kerb cairn (no. 10).

Recent geophysical survey suggests that these stones may once have been part of a much larger complex of monuments and earthworks.

Access to sites nos. 8–12

Nos. 8-12 are reached from a car-park 1.6 miles south of Kilmartin, signposted Dunchraigaig cairn. There you will find an interpretation panel describing all the monuments within view; further panels are at the sites themselves. A management agreement between Historic Scotland and the landowner is currently in place, which enables free public access to Ballymeanoch stones, henge and kerb cairn (nos. 8–10). Dunchraigaig cairn (no. 11) and Baluachraig carvings (no. 12) are in the care of Historic Scotland.

Ballymeanoch stones

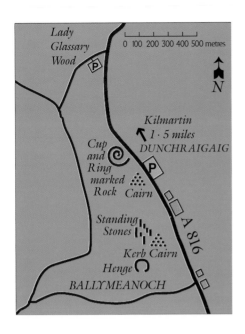

9. Ballymeanoch henge *NR 833 962*

This is the only henge monument in the west of Scotland. A henge consists of a circular bank of earth with internal ditch and either one or two gaps or entrances. This one had two entrances, but the monument is now difficult to see clearly.

The henge was probably built in about 3,000 BC–2,500 BC. We do not know how it was used at first, but in about 2,000 BC people used the space for burial of the dead. Two burial cists were found within the henge, one containing a decorated Beaker. This pot belongs to the British Museum but is currently on display in Kilmartin House Museum (see p 63).

(Access–see no. 8)

10. Ballymeanoch kerb cairn *NR 833 964*

Originally this burial cairn was circular, with kerb stones forming a ring all the way round, as at Temple Wood (no. 6). Only 11 kerbstones and several stumps remain and much of the cairn material has been taken for other purposes. The kerbstones are graded in height with the tallest on the SW. The cairn has not been excavated but similar monuments in Argyll date to about 1300 BC.

(Access–see no. 8)

Ballymeanoch henge

11. Dunchraigaig cairn *NR 833 968*

This burial cairn lies on ground slightly raised above the valley floor. It was examined both in the 1860s and in the 1920s. A curious mixture of burial practices were uncovered at the site. In about 2000–1500 BC people had laid a body on the ground, above which a cist or stone coffin had been built. The cremated remains of several individuals were found in the cist accompanied by a finely decorated pot. Above the cist a further body was laid 'gone almost entirely to decay' by the time it was uncovered in 1864. Another decorated pot and some burnt bones were found in another cist under the cairn material, and in a third cist, still visible today, people had placed both cremated and unburnt bones.

The two pots are in the National Museum of Scotland.

(Access–see no. 8)

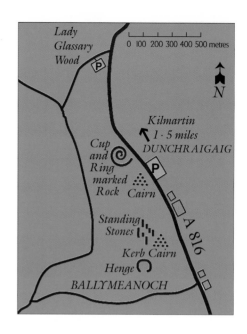

Kilmichael Carvings ▶

Dunchraigaig Cairn

12. Baluachraig carvings *NR 831 969*

Three sections of bedrock, in an enclosure slightly above Kilmartin valley floor, are decorated with prehistoric cup–and–ring marks. These consist of hollows or cups surrounded by a variable number of rings. In this case there are 17 cups with double rings, 16 cups with single rings and at least 138 simple cups.

There is an impressive concentration of such carvings in the area. Their purpose is not known. (Access–no. 8)

Achnabreck Carvings ▶

Baluachraig Carvings

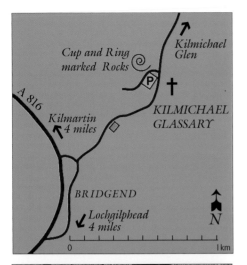

13. Kilmichael carvings *NR 857 934*

The prehistoric carvings on this outcrop include some unusual motifs such as four cups surrounded by keyhole shaped grooves and a firm line meandering from the radius of one ring to form part of the keyhole design around a cup a metre away. There are many cup marks, several surrounded by rings and some with grooves radiating from the cups.

Part of a second group of carvings can be seen outside the fenced area, about 60m to the NNE. It comprises the more standard motifs of simple cups surrounded by rings and includes one cup with 5 rings and 1 cup with 4.

Access

About 4·5 miles south of Kilmartin on the A 816, take the turning NE to Kilmichael Glassary. Follow the signs to Kilmichael Glen. Opposite Kilmichael church and before leaving the village, turn left into an area of housing. Almost immediately you will see a small parking area, opposite which is the enclosed area of carvings.

Kilmichael carvings are in the care of Historic Scotland.

14. Achnabreck carvings *NR 855 906/857 906/856 905*

The decorated outcrops at Achnabreck form the most extensive group of pre-historic carvings in Scotland. The most common motif is a hollow or cup surrounded by up to seven rings, often with a gutter running from the cup outwards. Other figures include spirals, multiple rings, peltas, ringed stars and parallel grooves. Some motifs, such as the spiral, may be compared to Irish passage grave art and may represent an earlier phase of carving.

Two separate outcrops can be visited at Achnabreck. The first you will reach is the most extensive and consists of three distinct groups of carvings. The second, though still impressive, is less profusely carved; it lies 150m away to the east.

Access

Near the Cairnbaan and Crinan turning off the A 816 (about 6 miles south of Kilmartin, 2 miles north of Lochgilphead) take the signposted track NE to Achnabreck. A car park is clearly signed after about half a mile. From there it is a 485m walk to the carvings. Achnabreck carvings are in the care of Historic Scotland.

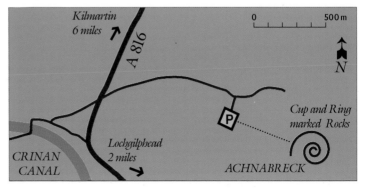

15. Cairnbaan carvings *NR 839 910/838 910*

Two groups of prehistoric carvings lie on a hill above Cairnbaan. One group includes several contiguous motifs with cups and multiple rings as well as irregular stretches of grooving and a figure resembling a star. The other includes at least 60 plain cup marks and several stretches of grooving as well as more unusual figures such as a double cup surrounded by a single ring.

Access

The carvings are behind the Cairnbaan hotel, which is on the B 841 near where it branches off the main A 816 (about 2 miles north of Lochgilphead and about 6 miles south of Kilmartin). To the east of the hotel, there are signposts to the carvings from where it is a threequarter mile walk. Cairnbaan carvings are in the care of Historic Scotland.

16. Ormaig carvings *NM 822 027*

Much of this outcrop of carvings was only exposed in 1974 so the carvings are relatively unweathered. It includes the usual hollows or cups surrounded by rings but also a rosette motif and a large cup surrounded by smaller cups. There was a fine outlook NW onto Loch Craignish, but this is increasingly obscured by trees (see photo p 64).

Access

The best way to reach this site is by bicycle, as the carvings lie several miles from Kilmartin along a forestry track (vehicles not permitted).

Ormaig carvings lie on Forest Enterprise land. A cycle route is marked from the car park at Carnassarie Castle, about 2 miles north of Kilmartin. Alternatively follow the ensuing directions from Kilmartin itself. As you leave Kilmartin in a northerly direction take the first turning to the left, immediately after an old filling station. When you reach the gravel quarry bear left along a new forestry road. Stay on this track until, about 2 miles from where you turned off the main road, you will see a turning on the right (sometimes with a chain across). Take this turning. After nearly 1.5 miles you will reach a locked gate. The carvings are about half a mile away. The track continues down hill towards the sea, and soon you will reach a sharp hairpin bend. In a short distance you will come to a small bridge over a stream. Cross the bridge and turn right off the track, upstream.

Follow an overgrown path, and after about 110 paces look to the left. This is where the carvings are, but there is a steep bank and the forestry is dense so you have to continue along the stream and double back. Continue for about 60 paces. Here the path starts to leave the stream and there is sometimes a wet flush here where water has run off the hill. Turn left (uphill) and take about 12 paces until, on your left, you will see a straight passage through the trees to a clearing. Take this , and after about 60 paces you will be in an open area where the carvings are located. They are near where you enter the clearing, a little to your right.

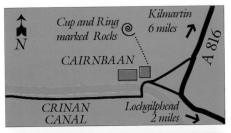

Cairnbaan Carvings

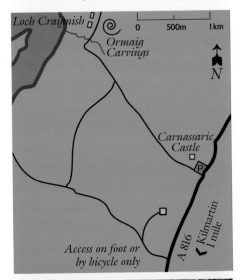

Ormaig Carvings

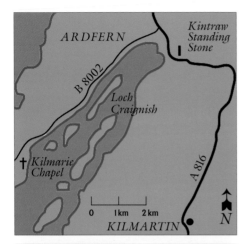

Kintraw Standing Stone

Castle Dounie

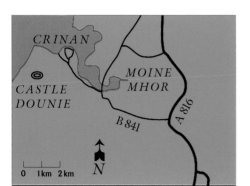

17. Kintraw standing stone and cairn NM 830 049
This group of monuments comprises two cairns, an enclosure and a 4m high stone.

Excavation in 1959–60 of one of the cairns revealed a kerb of stones incorporating a 3 slab setting or false portal (see p 69). The cairn may originally have been capped with quartz, and a timber post once stood in its centre. Jet beads lay within the only cist.

The stone fell in 1978-9 and was not aligned correctly when re-erected. Several theories regarding the site's possible astronomical significance have been put forward. The site overlooks Loch Craignish and the Sound of Jura.

Access
Kintraw is on the A 816 about 6 miles north of Kilmartin on a steep winding piece of road known as the Bealach. It is on the right of the road as you descend the hill going north to Oban.

The monument is on private land.

18. Castle Dounie NR 767 932
This unusual dun has extensive views over the Sound of Jura. Interesting architectural features include an extra skin of walling on the east side incorporating two chambers. Another chamber is at the SE corner. There is some evidence for a corbelled roof and for a stairway within the east wall.

Access
Follow the signs off the A 816 to Crinan. Before reaching the village of Crinan itself take a left hand turning signposted to Crinan harbour. If you have a car, swing to the right when you reach the sea and continue until you see a car park on your right. If on foot or with a bicycle do not swing right, but follow a path to the left which follows the shore line and then turns uphill. There are Forest Enterprise signs, but it is advisable to take a map and a compass. The site is on land owned by Forest Enterprise.

19. Dunadd *NR 837 935*

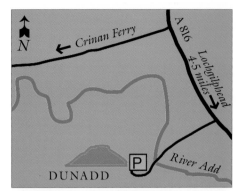

Dunadd fort stands on a rocky hill in the middle of one of the last remaining raised bogs in Scotland–the Mòine Mhór or Crinan Moss. The site has been excavated several times, most recently in the 1970s when radiocarbon dates and many finds show the site to have been used between the 6th and 10th centuries AD.

The fort was occupied by the Scotti who later gave their name to modern Scotland. They came from Ireland during the 5th–6th century AD. The dominating architecture, the rich finds– including evidence of fine metal-working, and of luxury goods imported from the continent – and the intriguing carvings, show that Dunadd was once an important, prestigious and well-connected place.

The carvings comprise a boar which in some respects resembles Pictish carvings of 7th–8th centuries, and an inscription in ogham, a form of writing used both by the Picts and the Scots. Until recently the carving has been described as Pictish but new research suggests it may be a commemorative inscription in Early Irish. The other two carvings – a rock-cut basin and a carved footprint – may have been used in early inauguration ceremonies. Footprint carvings are known in Britain from the Iron Age onwards and are recorded in such ceremonies in the Mediaeval period in Scotland.

Access

The signposted turning to Dunadd is on the A 816, 3.5 miles south of Kilmartin. A track about a third of a mile long takes you to a car park at the foot of the hill. From there it is a short walk to the summit.

Dunadd is the care of Historic Scotland.

Dunadd

20. Old Parish Church, Kilmarie, Craignish *NM 778 014*

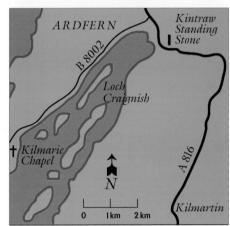

This former parish church probably dates to the 13th century though much repair is more recent. It overlooks Loch Craignish and neighbours ruins of a former township, Kirkton. Its dedication was to St. Maelrubha of Applecross. The church contains a collection of Medieval slabs which formerly were in the graveyard.

Most of the carved stones are products of the 14th–15th century Loch Awe School. They depict crosses, swords, armoured figures in niches, and are mostly carved in local epidiorite or quartzitic gneiss. Some are of Easdale slate. There are also some Early Christian slabs (pre 10th century) and some 16th century stone chests.

An epidiorite cross base is carved with a sundial; it has a central socket and 24 rays with cardinal points marked by crosses.

Access

Six miles north of Kilmartin on the A 816 take a left turn along the B 8002 to Ardfern. You will come to the village after 1 mile. The chapel is a further 3 miles on the left.

Kilmarie Church is in private ownership.

Old Parish Church, Craignish

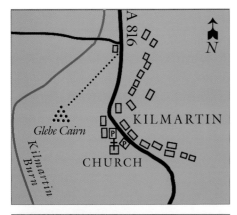

21. Kilmartin Church *NR 834 988*

Built in 1836 the current church replaces an earlier building of 1798 and one earlier still of 1601. The earliest suggestion of a church in Kilmartin is in 1323 with a record of the 'vicar of Kilmartin'. The current church and churchyard contain one of the most extensive collections of Mediaeval graveslabs in Western Scotland, many the products of the 14th–15th century Loch Awe School, with depictions of swords, crosses, and armoured figures. There are almost no inscriptions, so little is known of their social context; one slab, now lost, commemorates Patrick, son of Gilchrist MacKeller. Words such as Poltalloch and Duntroon, carved into the Mediaeval stones, are much later additions. Similar stones, and others from the Iona and Loch Sween Schools, can be found at Kilmarie Church (no. 20), Kilmichael Church (NR 859 935), Kilmory Knap chapel (NR 702 751), Old Parish Church, Kilneuair (NM 889 036) and Keills chapel (NR 691 805).

There are three Early Christian slabs in the churchyard, and a finely decorated cross in the church probably dates to the 9th or 10th century.

Access

The church is in the village of Kilmartin on the A 816. There is a car park immediately outside. When the church is locked a key can be obtained from no. 16 Kilmartin.

Mediaeval slabs, Kilmartin Churchyard

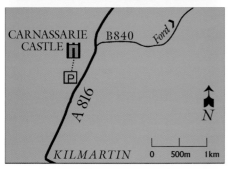

22 Carnassarie Castle *NM 839 008*

Carnassarie Castle was built between 1565 and 1572 for John Carswell, Bishop of the Isles. In 1567 Carswell translated the Book of Common Order, the earliest printed book in Scots Gaelic. From 1643 the castle was held by the Campbells of Auchenbreck and, as a result of Sir Duncan Campbell's support of the Earl of Argyll's rising in 1685, it was besieged, partly blown up and set on fire. The castle was not subsequently repaired.

The castle comprises a three-storey tower to the east, a four-storey stair tower and a three-storey hall. The building has been consolidated by Historic Scotland and is well-preserved, with elaborate stone carving remaining intact.

Access

Follow the A 816 north from Kilmartin. On the left hand side after about 2 miles you will see a signposted car park. From there it is about a half mile walk. If you are on a bicycle you can ride all the way to the castle.

Carnassarie Castle is in the care of Historic Scotland.

Carnassarie Castle

GLOSSARY

Beaker   A type of pottery vessel used throughout Europe from the mid 3rd millennium BC to the early 2nd millennium BC. Decoration is abstract and geometric and is made with incisions, and impressions of twisted cord, reeds, shells etc. Many are very finely made.

Cairn   A pile of stones, deliberately placed. Small ones may simply mark routeways, and others are the result of field clearance, but in an archaeological context the term usually implies burial beneath the stones.

Celtic   A term most usefully used to describe a group of connected languages. It is the first language we know people spoke in Scotland. Within Britain there are 2 distinct groups: Brittonic (P-Celtic) consisting of Welsh, Cornish and Breton, and Goidelic (Q-Celtic) consisting of Gaelic (Irish and Scottish) and Manx. In 1st millennium AD Britain the various Celtic-speaking people did not necessarily feel any sort of group identity, nor did they themselves use the term Celtic.

Chambered cairn   A cairn (see above) containing stone-built chambers in which people placed the remains of the dead, sometimes over several generations. They were first used in Scotland in about 4,000 BC and continued to be built until the 3rd millennium BC. They were often reused later.

Cist   A grave built with stone slabs. These are found both within cairns (see above) and uncovered, sometimes in groups.

Crannog   A dwelling built on an artificial island.

Cup and ring mark   A carving in rock consisting of a hollow surrounded by one or more rings, sometimes with a groove or gutter leading outwards from the cup. They occur on bedrock, on boulders and on monuments. They could date from the 4th to the 2nd millennium BC but most probably date to between 2,500 and 1,500 BC.

Dun   An area on a hill-top fortified by stone walls. The term is used to describe a smaller area than that implied by the term Fort (see below). Few have been excavated so dating is uncertain. Dates probably range from 600 BC to AD 800.

Earthworks   Monuments built of earth. The nature of the material means they rarely survive and are often known through aerial photographs or geophysical survey.

Food vessel   A type of decorated pottery used in Britain and Ireland in the first half of the second millennium BC. Various shapes are incorporated within this term, from vases to bowls.

Fort   In archaeology this usually implies a fortified hill-top dwelling of a reasonable size – big enough for various buildings to be within the walls rather than just a single dwelling. Dating is the same as Duns (see opposite) though there are some examples of forts, especially in southern England, which are much earlier.

Geophysical survey   An investigation which examines features underground without excavation. This can be done by testing electrical resistance, for example.

Henge   A monument of uncertain function consisting of a circular area enclosed by a bank and ditch with one or two openings. They date from between about 3,500 and 2,500 BC but were often reused later.

Ogham   A form of writing originating in Ireland in the 4th century AD. It consists of groups of incised lines, usually on stone, but also on wood and bone.

Picts   A term used (from about 4th century AD onwards) for the people who lived north of the River Forth. The people did not necessarily feel all part of the same group and did not use the term to describe themselves. They spoke P-Celtic (see above under Celtic), but left no writing.

Post hole   The trace in the ground of where a post has been. The soil is of a different character than that surrounding it, and packing stones are often present. Groups of post holes can show where buildings once have been.

Radiocarbon dating   A method of dating which measures the amount of radiocarbon in organic substances. This decays at a steady rate once the subject has died enabling an estimate of the date of death to be made.

Scotti   A term for the people living in Ireland and western Scotland in the first millennium AD. They spoke Gaelic – a Q-Celtic language (see above under Celtic).

NOTES

Books and journals are referred to in full unless they appear in the Further Reading (p 108) in which case only the author's name and the date of publication will be given. The following abbreviations are used: **PSAS** Proceedings of the Society of Antiquaries of Scotland; **OSA** Statistical Account of Scotland, 1791-9, Edinburgh; **NSA** New Statistical Account of Scotland, 1845; **GAJ** Glasgow Archaeological Journal; **Argyll 6** RCAHMS (1988) *Argyll: an Inventory of the Ancient Monuments. Vol 6: Mid Argyll and Cowal: Prehistoric and Early Historic Monuments*, Edinburgh; **Argyll 7** RCAHMS (1992) *Argyll: an Inventory of the Ancient Monuments. Vol 7: Mid Argyll and Cowal: Medieval and Later Historic monuments*, Edinburgh.

NB The numbers given for monuments in Argyll 6 also apply to RCAHMS (1999a) *Kilmartin-Prehistoric and early historic monuments: an inventory of the monuments extracted from Argyll volume 6.*

TIME AND LANDSCAPE

p 10-11 KILMARTIN'S LANDSCAPE

1. The last cold stage in Britain is known as the Devensian glaciation with the main phase of glacier expansion occurring in the Late Devensian from about 25,000 years ago and reaching its height between 23,000 and 20,000 years ago. The brief warming period (the Devensian Lateglacial Interstadial) was followed by the Loch Lomond Stadial- known as the Younger Dryas Stadial in Europe. For a map of Britain showing the maximum extents of the Loch Lomond and Late Devensian glaciers see Bell M and Walker M J C (1992) *Late Quaternary Environmental Change*, Harlow p 84. For an argument that ice in the Loch Lomond Stadial reached beyond Loch Awe into the valley between Ford and Kilmartin see Tipping R (1989). Palynological evidence for the extent of the Loch Lomond Readvance in the Awe Valley and adjacent areas, SW Highlands, *Scottish Journal of Geology*, 25, p 325-337. See also Gray J M (1992) Glacial Geology and Geomorphology, in Walker M J C, Gray J M and Lowe J J (eds) (1992).
2. The complexities of terrace formation are not yet fully understood. See Gray J M (1992) Ford to Kilmartin: Glaciofluvial Geomorphology, in Walker M J C, Gray J M and Lowe J J (eds) (1992) p 127-132 and Tipping R (1999) Kilmartin Valley landforms and landscape evolution, in RCAHMS (1999a).
3. For an overview of climatic change see Lowe J J (1993) Setting the scene: an overview of climatic change, in Smout T (ed) (1993) p 1-16, and Whittington G and Edwards K (1997) Climate change, in Edwards K and Ralston I (eds) (1997)

p 11-22. See also Sutherland D (1997) The Environment of Argyll, in Ritchie G (ed) (1997) p 10-24. For more of a focus on Kilmartin see Tipping in RCAHMS (1999a)- see above n.2. Climatic change inferred from the Greenland ice core is described by Mayewski P, Buckland P, Edwards K, Meeker L and O'Brien S (1996) in Pollard T and Morrison A (eds) (1996).
4. Tipping R (1992) Early Flandrian pollen sites in the Awe valley, in Walker M J C, Gray J M and Lowe J J (eds) (1992). Rymer L (1977) A Late-glacial and early Post-glacial pollen diagram from Drimnagall, North Knapdale, Argyllshire, *New Phytologist*, 79, p 211-221. For summary of Rymer's results see his articles in *The Kist* (journal of the Natural History and Antiquarian Society of Mid Argyll) 11 p 1-9, and 12 p 8-16.
5. Remains of arctic or collared lemming (*Dicrostonyx torquatus*) were found, for example, at Corstorphine, Edinburgh-see Sutcliffe A J and Kowalski K (1976) Pleistocene vertebrates of the British Isles, *Bulletin of the British Museum Natural History (Geology)* 27 p 33-147. Lemming remains were also found in the Creag nan Uamh caves in Assynt. The initial report is Callander, Cree and Ritchie (1927) Preliminary report on caves containing Palaeolithic relics, near Inchnadamph, Sutherland, *PSAS* 61 p 169-72; the site has subsequently been much discussed because of the presence of at least 900 reindeer antlers and the possibility that their deposition might represent evidence for very early human settlement in Scotland. For summary of the debate, and references to more recent articles see Morrison A and Bonsall C (1990) The Early Post Glacial Settlement of Scotland: A review, in Bonsall C (ed.) (1990) *The Mesolithic in Europe* p 136-7.

p 12-13 CONSTRUCTING THE PAST

6. NSA p 555-6.
7. Thomas F W L (1878) Dunadd, Glassary, Argyllshire: the place of inauguration of the Dalriadic Kings, *PSAS* 13 p 28-47. Argyll 6 no. 248. Argyll 7 no. 281.

p 14-15 HISTORY IN CONTEXT

TEMPERATURE

Past temperatures are estimated using a variety of techniques: the study of plant and animal remains, inferring temperature from presence or absence of cold and hot loving species; the analysis of assemblages of plankton such as diatoms or foraminifera which indicate specific water temperatures; the analysis of the isotopic records of micro-organisms within the ocean water column; analysis of sediments within ice cores. See Lowe J J (1993) Setting the Scene- an overview of climatic change, in Smout T C (ed) (1993), Aberdeen p 1-16 for an explanation of some of these techniques.

The fluctuating temperature line shown on the chart was drawn up following discussion with Richard Tipping. See Tipping R, Carter S and Haggart B A (forthcoming) *The recent evolution of Scotland's landscapes*. It takes into account the recent work with ice cores (see ref in note 3 p 10-11). Other authorities

(eg Edwards K in Edwards K J and Ralston I B M (eds) (1997) argue that temperatures over the past 7,000 years have been more stable.

Note that there are no figures given; the line shows relative temperatures.

CHANGING SEA LEVELS

Data from work by various researchers have been used to produce this indication of probable sea levels –work for example by Alastair Dawson on Islay and Jura (see his The raised shorelines of northern Islay and western Jura, in *Scottish Geographical Magazine* vol 107 no 3 p 207-212 (1991)). The curve on the time-line attempts to give a general picture for Argyll, which is impossible because the sea level varied from place to place because of the different timing and extent of the land's rebound.

A graph and summary of recent research on the changing sea levels in Argyll is given in Sutherland D G (1997) The Environment of Argyll, in Ritchie G (ed) (1997). See also Gray J M (1992) Raised Shorelines, in Walker M J C, Gray J M and Lowe J J (eds) (1992).

PLANTS

This generalized picture has been produced by Kevin Edwards and derives from the work of various researchers in several locations around Kilmartin. The following are some of the studies of local pollen cores:

Tipping R M (1989) Devensian Lateglacial vegetation history of Loch Barnluasgan, Argyllshire, western Scotland, *J. Biogeogr.*, 16 p 435-47; Tipping R M (1992) Early Flandrian pollen sites in the Awe valley, in Walker M J C, Gray J M and Lowe J J (eds) (1992) p 135-141; Rymer L (1977) A Late-glacial and early Post-glacial pollen diagram from Drimnagall, North Knapdale, Argyllshire, *New Phytologist*, 79, p 211-221; Haggart B and Sutherland D (1992) Móine Mhór, also in Walker M J C et al (1992) p 143-152.

FAUNA

Much of the data presented here is educated guesswork; animal remains only rarely survive so the earliest physical remains of a wolf, for example, date to long after its probable arrival. Extinctions are equally problematic. In the case of the beaver, for example, its most recent physical evidence dates to 1550 AD, but there is oral tradition of survival until the beginning of the 19th century. See Kitchener A (1998) Extinctions, Introductions and Colonisations of Scottish Mammals and Birds since the Last Ice Age in Lambert R(ed) (1998) *Species History in Scotland*, Edinburgh.

EVENTS

Most of these are relatively well attested though there is always scope for developments being moved back in time due to new discoveries and increasingly sophisticated dating techniques; cave paintings dated recently from Cosquer (Bouches-du-Rhone), for example, were 30,000 years old–10,000 years earlier than estimated (see Bahn P and Vertut J (2nd ed. 1997) *Journey Through the Ice Age*, London). Features such as cup-and-ring carvings are impossible to date exactly and were used over many thousands of years, so there will always be room for interpretation. Monuments such as the pyramids will always be subject to speculation; a recent (very controversial) theory suggests that the pyramids should be pushed back to 10,500 BC (Hancock G and Faiia S 1998 *Quest for the Lost Civilization*, London.).

p 16–17 TELLING THE TIME

8. Argyll 1 no 57
9. Argyll 6 no 364. Gladwin P F (1985) *The Solar Alignment at Brainport Bay, Minard, Argyll*, Natural History and Antiquarian Society of Mid Argyll
10. The bronze calendar measures 5 feet x 3 feet 6 inches and is engraved with a calendar of 62 lunar months. It can be seen in the Musée Archaeologique de Fourviere, Lyons. Early writers who mention the Celts' calendrical skills include Strabo, Caesar and Hecateus. See Piggott S (1994–first published 1968) *The Druids*, London p 115–7.
11. A good general book discussing the history of calendar making is Duncan, D E (1998) *The Calendar*, London.
12. The Synod of Whitby AD 664. For an account by the English monk Bede (673-735) see his *A History of the English Church and People*, book 3 chapter 25 (p 188–192 in Penguin edition 1981).
13. Thom A (1967) *Megalithic sites in Britain*, Oxford; Thom A (1971) *Megalithic Lunar Observatories*, Oxford. Thom A and Thom A (1978) *Megalithic Remains in Britain and Brittany*, Oxford. MacKie 1974 Archaeological tests on supposed astronomical sites in Scotland, *Philosophical Transactions of the Royal Society of London* A 276 1974 p 169– 194. A lucid introduction to the subject is Burl A (1997–first published 1983) *Prehistoric astronomy and ritual*, Aylesbury. See also MacKie E W (1977) *Science and Society in Prehistoric Britain*, London.

p 18–19 SEEING THE LANDSCAPE

14. Campbell M and Sandeman M (1962) p 62 no. 400. Byrne K (1997) *Colkitto*, Colonsay p 178f. For a poetic account of the event see Campbell M (1995–first pub. 1977) *Argyll: the Enduring Heartland*, Grantown-on-Spey p 125–127

p 20–21 READING THE LANDSCAPE

15. Argyll 6 no 211; Haggart B A and Sutherland D G (1992) The Mòine Mhór, in Walker M J C, Gray J M and Lowe J J (eds) (1992). The chronology of peat formation on the Mòine Mhór is still poorly understood, but work is currently (1999) underway to build up a clearer picture. For case studies of soil changes see Foster S and Smout T C (eds) (1994) *The History of Soils and Field Systems*.
16. The original documentation concerning the agricultural improvements on the Poltalloch Estate is held by Argyll and Bute Council's archivist in Lochgilphead, Argyll. See also Michael Davis's book on Poltalloch (forthcoming).
17. 74% of woodland in Argyll is exotic conifer plantation–124,836 of a total of 168,625 hectares (1998

figures by Caledonian Partnership based on analysis of aerial photographs).

p 22–23

18. Temple Wood–Argyll 6 no. 228
19. Argyll 6 no. 213. For mention of Kilmichael Tryst see Campbell M and Sandeman M (1962) p 92 no. 563. The cairns and circles are described by Simpson J Y (1868) On ancient sculpturings of cups and concentric rings etc, *PSAS* 6 Appendix p 37. 'Three large cairns' are mentioned, and it is said that three 'circles and cairns' lying in an adjacent field had been destroyed by gunpowder.

p 24–25

20. *Origines Parochiales Scotiae* (1851-5), Bannatyne Club p 92-3. The Charter is reproduced in Donaldson G (1997–first pub 1970) *Scottish Historical Documents*, Glasgow p 51
21. OSA p 249.

p 26–27

22. The house is now ruined and inaccessible to the public. See Argyll 7 no.177. It was built in 1850s by William Burn under directions from Neill Malcolm (III) and his wife Louisa Shirley. It was an expensive mansion even by the standards of the time; tourists passing through Crinan Canal were told it cost £100,000 –a colossal sum. (Info from MS of Michael Davis's book on Poltalloch Estate –publication forthcoming.)
23. Survey by Robert Monleith 1824, Poltalloch papers, Argyll and Bute Council archives Dr/2/12.

p 28–29

24. Argyll 6 no. 109. Recently (1997) more discoveries have been made, including evidence for a possible 45m diameter timber circle and cursus monument. See *Discovery and Excavation in Scotland* 1997 p 19-21, published by Council for Scottish Archaeology.
25. These differing values are not necessarily compatible, as has become apparent in recent debates about the fate of this quarry.
26. Argyll 6 no. 68. Campbell M and Sandeman M (1962) p 17 no. 114. Craw J H (1931) Further Excavation of Cairns at Poltalloch, Argyll *PSAS* 65 p 269–275.
27. Old Parish Church, Kilmarie, Craignish–Argyll 7 no. 67.
28. MacTavish Duncan C (ed) (1943) *Minutes of the Synod of Argyll 1639–1661* (2 vols), Edinburgh vol 1 p 186 (16th Oct 1650).

p 30–31

29. MacTavish Duncan C (ed) (1943) *Minutes of the Synod of Argyll 1639–1661* (2 vols), Edinburgh vol 1 p 104 (12 Oct 1647) and vol 1 p 193 (16th Oct 1650).
30. Argyll 7 no. 115. Carnassarie Castle is also among the castles described in RCAHMS (1998).
31. Duncan Campbell of Auchinbreck was a member of one of Argyll's most powerful families of the day. Carnassarie Castle was among his properties. His principal residence was at Lochgair (see Argyll 7 no 136) which also was plundered in 1685. Duncan

Campbell was a supporter of the uprising in May 1685 of the 9th Earl of Argyll. It ended in failure and Argyll was executed on June 30th 1685. For more information about the Campbells of Auchinbreck see Fraser A (1964) *North Knapdale in the 17th and 18th centuries*, Oban.
32. NSA p 556.
33. MacTavish D C (ed 1935) *The Commons of Argyll –Name-Lists of 1685 and 1692*, Lochgilphead [77 men are listed from Kilmartin as fighting with Argyll in 1685 of which 43 are recorded as having subsequently forfeited goods eg
Dougald mcOllvorie in Arhamsh lost 9 cows and 1 horse
Martin mcIllgurine in Achinellan lost 3 cows, 2 horses and 5 sheep
Donald mcIllgallachlich in Ellanrie lost 2 cows
Dugald mcLaertich in Slugane lost 2 cows
Duglad mcInvaine in Ardfure lost 4 cows and 1 mare
John mcPhaiden in Culchruck (=Cowlchrowk) lost 15 cows, 2 horses and 1 mare
Dugald Roy Campbell in Carnasarie lost 1 cow
Total number of animals seized from Kilmartin parish as a punishment for the rebellion (declared at Court held by the Marquis of Atholl at Inveraray on 12th Oct 1685): 177 cows, 14 horses, 7 mares, 7 sheep.
146 men are listed from Glassary as fighting with Argyll in 1685 eg
Allan mcLauchlane of Dunad forfeited 12 cows, 2 horses and 3 mare.
Alexander ffergusone in Stronalbanich forfeited 10 cows, 1 horse and 1 mare].

p 32–33

34. Pennant T (First pub. 1774 & 1776) *A Tour in Scotland and voyage to the Hebrides 1772*, Chester. In 1998 edition (Simmons A (ed), Edinburgh) see p 204-5.

CLOSE TO THE WIND

p 35

1. A list of radiocarbon dates for Argyll is given in Ashmore P (1997): Radiocarbon dates from archaeological sites in Argyll and Arran, in Ritchie G (ed) (1997) (1997) p 236–283, including calibrated dates for hazelnuts at Staosnaig, Colonsay, antler points from Druimvargie rock shelter, Oban, and charcoal from lithic sites on Jura.
2. A graph and summary of recent research on the changing sea levels in Argyll is given in Sutherland D G (1997) The Environment of Argyll, in Ritchie G (ed) (1997). See also Gray JM (1992): Raised Shorelines, in Walker M J C, Gray JM and Lowe J J (1992), and notes above to p14-15.

p 36-7 CROSSING THE WATER

3. The carving shown is from Trondheimsfjord, peninsula Frosta, Evenhus, Norway.
4. Fenton A (1972) The Currach in Scotland with notes on the Floating of Timber, *Scottish Studies* vol 16 part 1, Aberdeen. The coracle shown here was made by Peter Faulkner Coracles, 24 Watling Street, Leintwardine, Shropshire.

5. Mowat R J C (1996) *The logboats of Scotland*, Oxford. A boat from Friarton, Perth is reported which may be earlier but it is the deposits in which it was found rather than the boat itself (which has not survived) from which a rough date (to the 6th millennium BC) is estimated–see Mowat p 34 no. 50.

6. A study of red deer on Oronsay suggests either that deer were hunted elsewhere and brought to the island, or that a population of deer had been introduced to the nearby, but bigger, island of Colonsay. Either way transport over water is implied. See Mellers P A (1987). The requirement for the small population of Oronsay to maintain contact with people elsewhere for breeding purposes also implies travel by sea. For discussions of ancient sea craft see McGrail S (1987) *Ancient boats in NW Europe: the archaeology of water transport to AD 1500*, London; Johnstone, P (1980) *The Sea-craft of Prehistory*, London.

7. Rufus Festus Avenius in *Ora Maritima*. The manuscript dates to AD 1488 and is thought to contain parts of the Massilote Greek Periplus. This may date to about the 6th century BC but it has been argued that the use of the term Oestrymnides for the waters around Britain implies a tradition going back before 1000BC. See Johnstone P (1980) *The Sea-craft of Prehistory*, London p 123.

8. The main reasons for the fierce nature of the waters among the islands are the following: the submarine topography, the difference in water level between the east and west sides of the Corryvreckan, and the differential in tidal cycle between the east and west sides of the island chain. The Corryvreckan between Jura and Scarba is a notorious series of whirlpools with a standing wave; it is to be avoided if possible. For the Sound of Jura, with tidal streams at springs of 6 to 8 knots, 'it is essential to work the tides unless you have a really hefty engine' (Lawrence 1994 p 7–see below). Its alternative name is An Linne Rosach or the Channel of Disappointment because of the strong tide and awkward seas. See Lawrence M (1993 & 1994–2 vols) *The Yachtsman's Pilot to the West Coast of Scotland, Clyde to Colonsay* (1993) and *Crinan to Canna* (1994).

p 38–9 MAKING BOATS

9. For more about the construction of skin boats see Johnstone P (1980) and McGrail S (1987) listed in note 6 above. See also the booklet on coracle construction (publication forthcoming) by Kilmartin House.

10. See map in Wickham-Jones C R (1994) p 54, for some of the possibilities. There is little consensus on the issue of where Scotland's first people came from, or indeed when.

p 40–41 LIVING FROM THE SHORE

11. For Oronsay see Mellers P A (1987). Evidence from the neighbouring island of Colonsay is summarised in Mithen S J (1996) The Southern Hebrides Mesolithic Project: Reconstructing Mesolithic Settlement in Western Scotland in Pollard T and Morrison A (1996). Risga was excavated in 1920–1 and the first report on the artefacts reported in Lacaille (1954) *The Stone Age in Scotland*, Oxford. Excavations in Oban are reported by Anderson J

(1895 and 1898) in *PSAS* nos. 29 and 32. Readable round ups of evidence from all these sites can be found in Wickham-Jones C R (1994), Smith C 1992 – *Late Stone Age Hunters of the British Isles*, London, and Bonsall C (1998) Coastal Adaptation in the Mesolithic of Argyll. Rethinking the 'Obanian Problem', in Ritchie G (ed) (1997) p 25–37.

12. Excavations on Jura are reported by Mercer J in *PSAS* 103, 104, 105 & 110.

13. Information on the human remains from Oronsay is given in Mellars P (1987) p 290–300, from which the photograph of the finger bone is taken. The map and the information on otoliths also comes from this work (p 2 and p 2-3 respectively). More detailed information on otoliths is reported in Mellars P A and Wilkinson M R (1980) Fish otoliths as indicators of seasonality in prehistoric shell middens: the evidence from Oronsay (Inner Hebrides), *Proceedings of the Prehistoric Society* 46 p 19–44.

p 42–43 USING THE PAST

14. There are several accounts of the history of archaeological thought eg Daniel G and Renfrew C (1988) *The Idea of Prehistory*, Edinburgh.

15. The term 'Obanian' was not generally used until the 1940s, though the idea of there being a distinct culture had first been suggested in the late 1890s following excavations of the main sites in Oban. The term and its usefulness or otherwise has been much discussed, in particular by Bonsall C (1992) The 'Obanian problem', in Pollard T and Morrison A (1992), and Bonsall C (1997) Coastal adaptation in the Mesolithic of Argyll. Rethinking the 'Obanian Problem', in Ritchie G (ed) (1997)

16. Mellars P A (1987)

17. Mellars P A (1987) p 153–181

18. Mellars P A (1987) p 117–126 with illustration of the lost antler points p119. Grieve's work on the Great Auk resulted in Grieve S (1885) *The Great Auk, or Garefowl* (Alca impennis, L): *its History, Archaeology and Remains*, London.

19. Andrews M V, Gilbertson D D, Kent M (1987) Storm Frequencies along the Mesolithic Coastline in Mellars PA (1987) p 108–114.

20. Oban Times, February 9, 1895.

p 44–45 THE RED DEER

21. These consist of part of the red deer skull with the antlers still attached, and were found at the Mesolithic site of Star Carr, Yorkshire. The very important series of excavations there is written up in Clark J G D (1971–second edition) *Excavations at Star Carr*, Cambridge. A summary, including an illustration of the perforated antlers, can be found in Smith C (1992) *Late stone age hunters of the British Isles*, London p 110–121.

22. Gundestrup Cauldron. See Kaul F, Marazov I, Best J, De Vries N (1991) *Thracian Tales on the Gundestrup Cauldron*, Amsterdam. See also Green M (1992) *Dictionary of Celtic Myth and Legend*, London (illustration from the Gundestrup Cauldron on front and p 29, description of the horned god Cernunnos p 59–61).

23. Both burials are from Vedbaek, Denmark. For illustrations see Wickham-Jones C R (1994) *Scotland's First Settlers*, London, pl. 10 (man with antlers), p 119 (child on swan's wing).

p 46 THE WOOD AGE

24. Edwards K and Ralston I (eds) (1997). Mellars P (1987).

25. The last wolf in Scotland was allegedly shot in AD 1743. The wild boar died out in the 16th or early 17th century. See Lambert Robert (ed) (1998) *Species History in Scotland*, Edinburgh. For one of the first, yet still influential, works which examines and laments the increasingly negative human impact on the environment see Carson R (1962) *Silent Spring*, London, the silence being the lack of bird song.

26. For a listing of the small quantity of prehistoric wood that has survived see Cole J, Heal S V E and Orme B J (1978) The use and character of wood in Prehistoric Britain and Ireland, *Proceedings of the Prehistoric Society* 44 p 1–45. An arrowshaft from Grampian was found to be of viburnum.

27. Drawing is from Wickham-Jones C R (1994) p 77. Original excavation report is Mercer J (1980) Lussa Wood 1: the Late-Glacial and Early Post-Glacial Occupation of Jura, *PSAS* 110 p 1-32.

28. Hamilton A, Bannon D, Monk M and Pals J P (1985) The botanical remains, in Woodman P C (1985) *Excavations at Mount Sandel 1973-77*, Belfast p 77–82.

p 47 MOVING THROUGH THE LANDSCAPE

29. Argyll 6 no. 357. The shelter shown in this photograph is now collapsed and dangerous.

30. Radiocarbon dates from bone artefacts from Druimvargie range from the second half of the 8th millennium BC to the first half of the 7th millennium BC–see Ashmore P (1997) Radiocarbon dates from archaeological sites in Argyll and Arran, in Ritchie G (ed) (1997).

31. The degree to which pre-farming people deliberately reduced tree cover is much debated. After about 4,000BC there is consensus that people did clear land for farming though the impact may have been quite small at first. See Edwards K and Ralston I (1984) Postglacial hunter-gatheres and vegetational history in Scotland, *PSAS* 114 (1984) p 15–34, and Edwards K and Whittington G (1997) Vegetation Change, in Edwards K J and Ralston I B M (eds) (1997).

BREAKING THE EARTH

p 48-49 MAKING MARKS

1. Argyll 6 no. 346. Rennie E B (1984) Excavations at Ardnadam, Cowal, Argyll 1964–1982 *GAJ* 11 p 13–39.

2. Connock K D, Finlayson B, Mills C M (1993) Excavation of a shell midden site at Carding Mill Bay near Oban, Scotland, *GAJ* 17 p 25–38.

3. Scott J G (1991) p 93–98.

4. Argyll 6 no. 350. Full publication forthcoming.

5. Ritchie A and Ritchie G, Whittington G and Soulsby J (1974) A Prehistoric field-boundary from the Black Crofts, North Connel, Argyll *GAJ* 3 p 66–70.

6. Haggarty A (1991) Machrie Moor, Arran: recent excavations at two stone circles *PSAS* 121 p 51–94.

p 50–51 HUNTING FOR NEW WAYS

7. The 7 chambered cairns, with their numerical entry in Argyll 6, are: Auchoish nr Achnabreck (8), Baroile at Rhudil (10), Upper Rhudil (21), Clach an t'Sagairt nr Ardfern (11), Gartnagreanoch nr Barnluasgan (16), Kilchoan (17), and Nether Largie South (19).
8. The boar is discussed extensively in Green M (1992) *Dictionary of Celtic Myth and Legend*, London.
9. Foster S M (1996) p 94.

p 52–53 STATUS FROM STONE

10. Clough T and Cummins W (eds) (1979 & 1988) *Stone Axe studies and Stone Axe studies 2*, CBA research reports, London.
11. Mitchell A (1884) On white pebbles in connection with pagan and Christian burial, a seeming survival of an ancient burial custom, *PSAS* 18.
p 286–291 summarises incidences of quartz in cairns in Argyll (Nether Largie South and Kilchoan included). The quantity of quartz at Kintraw (Argyll 6 no. 63) led the excavator to suggest that the cairn may once have had a quartz capping–see Simpson D D A (1968) Excavations at Kintraw, Argyll *PSAS* 99 p 54–59.
12. Edmonds M (1995) *Stone Tools and Society*, London, includes map (p 52) of distribution of axes from four different sources. The most thoroughly investigated site in Scotland is at Killin–see Edmonds M, Sheridan A and Tipping R (1992) Survey and excavation at Creag na Caillich, Killin, Perthshire, *PSAS* 122 p 77–112.
13. Saville A and Sheridan A (1990) The Campbeltown flint hoard *Past* 9 p 4–5.
14. The arrowheads are shown (from left to right) barbed and tanged, leaf and microlith. The earliest is the microlith used by Scotland's first settlers. The leaf is found in contexts dating from the 4th and 3rd millennia (earlier in Ireland) and the barbed and tanged arrow is typical of the late 3rd millennium BC onwards.
15. Argyll 6 no. 17.

p 54 VESSELS FROM THE EARTH

16 The illustration shows a selection of pots, all from 4-3rd millenium BC Scotland.
17 The original basket was found 3.5m deep in a bog at Twyford, County Westmeath, Ireland. Another basket from Ireland (from Aghintemple, Co. Longford) contained a polished axe.

p 55 HISTORY IN THE BOG

18 This generalised picture has been drawn up by Kevin Edwards using data from several sites around Kilmartin. See note under plants p 14–15.
19. In many species it is only possible to tell genera but not species. An introduction to the use of pollen in the reconstruction of ancient environments is Whittington G (1993), Pollen analysis as a tool for environmental history, in Smout T C (ed) 1993 p 28–39.

HEAVEN & EARTH

p 56
1. 2 cist sites in line with the others may originally have been covered by cairns. These are at Rowanfield (Argyll 6 no. 106) and Crinan Moss (Argyll 6 no. 88).
2. Jet for necklaces came from Whitby in Yorkshire, many of the Food Vessels are of a shape and style similar to that found in Ireland, and Beakers shared traits with pottery found in England and on the continent.
3. Argyll 6 no.222.

p 57 AN ORGANISED LANDSCAPE

4. Argyll 6 no. 228.
5. Gillies P H (1909) *Nether Lorn and its Neighbourhood* p 147-8.
6. Argyll 6 no. 109. cf p 28 note 23.

p 58-59 KILMARTIN IN 1,500 BC – THE LINEAR CEMETERY
7. Kilmartin Church–Argyll 7 no. 68.
8. Upper Largie–Argyll 6 no. 109. cf p 28 note 23. For a description of other timber circles in Britain see Gibson A (1998) *Stonehenge and Timber Circles*, Stroud.
9. Glebe cairn Argyll 6 no. 62; *PSAS* 6 (1864–6) p 339–41; Campbell M and Sandeman M (1962) p 16 no. 105.
10. Nether Largie North Argyll 6 no. 68; *PSAS* 65 (1930–1) p 269–74; Campbell M and Sandeman M (1962) p 17 no. 114, p 34 no. 243, p 38 no. 269.
11. Nether Largie Stones, Argyll 6 no. 222. A copy of Duncan Abernethy's Geophysics report is available for consultation in Kilmartin House.
12. Argyll 6 nos. 106 (Rowanfield) and 88 (Crinan Moss).
13. References to the cist excavations appear in Argyll 6 no. 104; Craw in *PSAS* 63 (1928–9) p 155–66; Campbell M and Sandeman M (1962) p 19 no. 129; Cregeen E in *GAJ* 8 (1981) p 19–28. The settlement site is described in Argyll 6 no. 350. The material is held by Glasgow Art Gallery and Museums; full publication is forthcoming.
14. Argyll 6 no. 67; *PSAS* 64 (1929-30) p127–30; Campbell M and Sandeman M (1962) p 17 no. 11.
15. Nether Largie South –Argyll 6 no. 19; *PSAS* 6 (1864-6) p 341-7; Henshall A S (1963 and 1972) *The Chambered Cairns of Scotland*, Edinburgh, vol 2 p 335-40; Campbell M and Sandeman M p 15 no. 95 (1962).
16. Ri Cruin–Argyll 6 no. 76; *PSAS* 8 (1868–70) p 378–81.

p 60 POWER HOLDERS

17. The Poltalloch necklace is on display in the Museum of Scotland. See Argyll 6 no. 104; Craw in *PSAS* 63 (1928–9) p 155-66; Sheridan A and Davis M (1995) The Poltalloch jet spacer plate necklace, *The Kist* (journal of the Natural History and Antiquarian Society of Mid Argyll) 49 p 1–9. For the Poltalloch halberd see *PSAS* 101 (1968–9) p 87, Campbell M and Sandeman M (1962) p 116 no. 24; there is an illustration in Clarke D V, Cowie T G and Foxon A (1985) *Symbols of Power at the time of Stonehenge*, Edinburgh p 97.

18. The richest source of jet in Britain is in Whitby, Yorkshire. As part of a project by the National Museums of Scotland, objects of jet and similar substances from all over Scotland have been analysed and, where possible, identified to source. Publication of the results is forthcoming.
19. Loch Melfort necklace is illustrated in Clarke D V, Cowie T G and Foxon A (1985) *Symbols of Power at the time of Stonehenge*, Edinburgh p 211, as are several other jet necklaces from Scotland. The finding of a similar necklace in Kintyre, Argyll is described by Peltenburg E J (1979) Two cist burials at Kintyre Nurseries, Campbeltown, Argyll, in *GAJ* 6 p 11–19. Morrison A (1979) A Bronze Age burial site at South Mound, Houston, Renfrewshire, also in *GAJ* 6 p 20–45 includes a list of all then-known jet necklaces in Scotland p 25–28.
20. The 12 grooved and rebated cists in the Kilmartin area are listed in Campbell M, Scott J G and Piggott S (1961) The Badden Cist Slab, *PSAS* 94 p 46–61.

p 61 GLEBE CAIRN

21. Glebe Cairn–Argyll 6 no. 62; Campbell M and Sandeman M p 16 no. 105; Greenwell in PSAS 6 (1864–6) p 339–41 from which comes the following extract:
' *The examination was commenced on the south-west side, when, about eight feet from the outside, some stones were found standing upright and apart. This proved to be a portion of one of a double circle of stones which was enclosed within the cairn*'.
22. The cairns are very dissimilar inside and their origins may not be contemporary. See the various accounts in Argyll 6.
23. Argyll 6 no. 228. The date of 3,000 BC is estimated from the possible date for the spiral carvings at Temple Wood, which can be compared with similar carvings on a macehead found at Knowth in Ireland; see Scott J G (1989).

p 62–63 BUILDING ON THE PAST

24. Argyll 6 no. 22, *PSAS* 6 (1864-6) p 348-9, Campbell M and Sandeman M (1962) p113 no. 12. Some important Scottish henges are at North Mains, Perthshire (*PSAS* 82 (1947–8) p68–123) and at Cairnpapple, West Lothian (*PSAS* 113 (1983) p 122–89). Both are illustrated in Barclay G (1998) *Farmers, Temples and Tombs: Scotland in the Neolithic and early Bronze Age*, Edinburgh. These and other henge monuments such as at Balfarg, Fife, and Stenness, Orkney are described in Ashmore P (1996).
25. Argyll 6 no. 19. The bones of several individuals are commonly represented in such tombs, but probably not enough to represent the remains of the whole community. Often only parts of bodies are present and the bones are disarticulated ie the flesh rotted off previous to burial. Bodies must have been 'exposed' before burial for this rotting process to take place; evidence for structures which might have been used for such a practice is sought by archaeologists but clinching evidence would be difficult to find. See Ashmore P (1996). The most comprehensive guide to chambered tombs in Scotland is Henshall A S (1963 and 1972) *The Chambered Cairns of Scotland*, Edinburgh.

p 64–65 CARVED ROCKS

26. Argyll 6 no. 179. For discussion of the unusual rosette designs see Van Hoek M A M (1993) The rosette in British and Irish rock art, *GAJ* 16 p 39–54.
27. 81 locations are described in Argyll 6, many of which consist of several outcrops. The small number of carvings in Kintyre and Lorn is covered in RCAHMS (1971) and RCAHMS (1975) respectively. See also Morris R W B (1977) *The Rock Art of Argyll*, Poole, and Stevenson J B *The Prehistoric Rock Carvings of Argyll* in Ritchie G (ed) (1997).
28. See Bradley R (1998) which describes similar rock carvings in Brittany, Portugal, Spain and Kilmartin. Carvings in Northumbria have been studied and described by Stan Beckensall; see Beckensall S (1983) *Northumberland's Prehistoric Rock Carvings*, Rothbury (Pendulum Press), Beckhensall S (1991 and 1992) *Prehistoric rock motifs of Northumberland – a complete guide: Vol 1 – Ford to Old Bewick, Vol 2 – Binley to the Tyne, Hexham* (available from author–address below). For Cumbria see Beckensall S (1992) *Cumbrian Prehistoric Rock Art. Symbols, Monuments and Landscape* (available from the author at 4 Leazes Crescent, Hexham, NE46 3JX). The publication of a new survey of British rock art is forthcoming: Beckensall S, *Prehistoric rock art in Britain*, Stroud and Charleston USA (Tempus publications).
29. A cup mark on a slab buried in a pit at Raigmore near Inverness is the earliest dated carving. Charcoal in the pit was dated to before 3,700 BC. There is a cup-and-ring mark and a cupmark on one of slabs within a chambered cairn at Ardmarnock in Cowal – see Argyll 6 no. 4; a date in the first half of the 3rd millennium BC is likely.
30. Ri Cruin – Argyll 6 no. 76. *PSAS* 8 (1868–70) p 378–81.
31. Achnabreck – Argyll 6 no. 113. See also Morris R W B (1974) The petroglyphs at Achnabreck, Argyll, *PSAS* 103 p 33–56.
32. The slighted cup mark is on one of two cists from Barsloisnoch – Argyll 6 no. 84. Badden cist slab: Argyll 6 no. 81; Campbell M Scott J G and Piggott S (1961) The Badden Cist Slab, *PSAS* 94 p 46–61.

p 65 HAVING THE EDGE

33. Copper daggers are mentioned by Greenwell in *PSAS* 6 (1864–6) p 346 & 350, and by Craw in *PSAS* 64 (1929–30) p 136.
34. Sites with axe carvings are Ri Cruin (Argyll 6 no. 76), Nether Largie Mid cairn (Argyll 6 no. 67), Nether Largie North cairn (Argyll 6 no. 68), and, possibly, Kilbride (Argyll 6 no. 98).
35. There is, for example, a large concentration of mines dating from between 1700 and 1500 BC at Mount Gabriel in West Cork, Ireland. See O'Brien W (1996) *Bronze Age Copper Mining in Britain and Ireland*, Princes Risborough (Shire pub.)

p 66-7 ALIGNMENT

36. Carbon date is 3794 BC from charcoal in a stone hole in the North circle at Temple Wood (calibrated date), but this date is not considered completely reliable. Regarding the stones at Ballymeanoch and Nether Largie, it could be argued that the carvings were made long before the stones were erected, but the carvings seem only to occur above the ground, suggesting either that they were carved with the use as standing stone in mind, or that the carvings were added later.
37. See note 13 to p 16 –17 (above).
38. Calculation by Eric Dudley of Map Maker Ltd, The Pier, Carradale, Kintyre. Tel. 01583 431 358. Web site is at www.mapmaker.com
39. For Temple Wood see Scott J G (1989) and Argyll 6 no. 228.
40. Argyll 6 no. 364. Gladwin, P Fane (1985) *The Solar Alignment at Brainport Bay, Minard, Argyll*, Natural History and Antiquarian Society of Mid Argyll.
41. Nether Largie stones – Argyll 6 no. 222. See note 13 p 16 –17 (above).

p 68–9 ORIENTATION

42. Kintraw – Argyll 6 no. 63. The site is described and illustrated in Burl A (1997) *Prehistoric Astronomy and Ritual*, Princes Risborough (Shire Publications) p 42-5. See also Patrick J (1981) A reassessment of the solsticial observatories at Kintraw and Ballochroy in Ruggles C and Whittle A (eds) *Astronomy and Society in Britain during the period 4000-1500 BC*, British Archaeological Reports no. 88 p 211-19.

p 70–71 BOGS AND METALWORK

43. The Shuna swords (now distributed between 3 museums – Kilmartin House (on loan from Fife District Museums Service), National Museums of Scotland, and Glasgow Art Gallery and Museum. They are illustrated together in RCAHMS (1975) pl. 5B. Their discovery is described in *PSAS* 11 (1874–6) p121 ('found within a short distance of each other, points downwards'). For references to the Torran Hoard see note 48 below.
44. After about 2,000 BC the climate became colder, windier and wetter but it is not clear which elements of landscape change are due to this, and which to do with human intervention. From this time heath and peat expanded with blanket bog and acid soils becoming increasingly abundant. See Sutherland D (1997) The Environment of Argyll in Ritchie (ed) (1997).
45. Kerb cairn, Ballymeanoch – Argyll 6 no. 31. A description of the excavation of several kerb cairns in Argyll is given in *PSAS* 106 (1974–5) p 30-3.
46. Cores taken from the Mòine Mhór are described by Haggart B and Sutherland (1992) Moine Mhor in Walker M J C, Gray, J M and Lowe J J (1992). Further work is underway.

p 72 OBJECTS IN THE LANDSCAPE

47. A survey of Scottish metalwork of this date is given by Coles J (1960) Scottish late bronze age metalwork: typology, distributions and chronology in *PSAS* 93 (1959–60) p16–134. The discovery of the Beith shields is given in *PSAS* 5 (1864) p 165 and *PSAS* 27 (1893) p 355–6, the latter including an illustration. The subject of hoards is dealt with by Bradley R (1990) *The Passage of Arms: an archaeological analysis of prehistoric hoard and votive deposits*, Cambridge (new edition by Oxbow 1998). Places of offering chosen by the Celts are discussed by Armit, I (1997) p 90 –94.

48. Argyll 6 p 27 (ill); *PSAS* 18 (1883–4) p 179, p 207–9; *PSAS* 19 (1884–5) p 53; *PSAS* 93 (1959–60) p 76, p 87, p 105; Campbell M and Sandeman M (1962) p 113.

p 73 MUSIC AND METALWORK

49. Note, for example, the similarity in style between Bronze Age pottery from Ireland and Argyll. For a discussion of some of the links between the two places see Moore D (ed) (1970) *The Irish Sea Province in Archaeology and History*, Cardiff.
50. For an account of experiments in making Bronze horns see Simon O'Dwyer's account in *Archaeology Ireland 2* (1988). For discussions of the horns see also Coles J in *Proceedings of the Prehistoric Society* 29 (1963). See also Purser J (1992) *Scotland's Music*, pub. by Mainstream.
51. The famous Irish epic tale, the Táin Bó Cuailnge (the Cattle Raid of Cooley), for example, revolves around a couple's desire each to own the most magnificent bull: Kinsella T (transl) (1969) *The Táin*, Oxford. See also the many references to the bull in Green M (1992) *Animals in Celtic Life and Myth*, London.

FRIENDS AND ENEMIES
p 76-7 SURVIVING ON A LOCH

1. Morrison I (1985). A reconstructed crannog is open to the public on Loch Tay near Kenmore (1 April–31October, 10am–5.30pm daily). Contact the Scottish Crannog Centre, tel. 01887 830 583, for further information.
2. Munro R (1882) *Ancient Scottish Lake Dwellings or Crannogs*, Edinburgh p 93. As quoted and illustrated in Morrison I (1985) p 96 –7.
3. Reverend Mapleton was the Episcopalian Dean of Argyll. He rented Duntroon Castle from Poltalloch Estate and excavated in Kilmartin valley at Ri Cruin cairn (*PSAS* 8 p 378–80, 1871), and Kilchoan chambered cairn (*PSAS* 6 p 351–5, 1866). He also investigated sites in the Fort William area.

p 78 ISLAND LANDSCAPE

4. Argyll 6 no. 352. *Kist* 5 (1973) p 2 –11. Morrison I (1985) figs. 3.2–3.4. The survey revealed many crannogs never before noted. No subsequent excavation has been carried. Carbon date for one of the crannogs is 370 BC ± 45 – Argyll 6 no. 352.4
5. A dwelling on an artificial island in Loch Olabhat, North Uist, for example, dates to the second half of the 4th millennium BC. An account of the crannogs in use into the 17th century is given in Morrison I (1985) p 22 –24.

p 79 ISLAND LODGE

6. Loch Glashan - Argyll 6 no. 354. Excavation report forthcoming. A natural island on Loch Glashan, with evidence for occupation in the late Medieval period, has also been excavated – see Argyll 7 no. 146, and Fairhurst H (1969) A medieval island-settlement in Loch Glashan, Argyll *GAJ* 1 (1969) p 47–67.
7. Leather finds included shoes and a jerkin. One small crucible was found, showing metal was worked on site. For an account of the impressive

range of wooden artefacts see Earwood C (1990) The wooden artefacts from Loch Glashan crannog, Mid Argyll *PSAS* 120 (1990) p 79–94.

p 80–1 A TENSE LANDSCAPE

8. See Argyll 6 and Campbell M and Sandeman M (1962) for full list. See also Ritchie (ed) (1997) p 118–180. The only ones excavated to date are Dunadd, Eilean Righ, Druim an Dùin, Duntroon and 2 which are not in fact on hilltops–Ardifuar , and Eilean an Dùin (Argyll 6 no. 258 and Nieke, M and Boyd W (1987) Eilean an Dùin, Craignish, Mid-Argyll, *GAJ* 14 p 48–53). For references to other reports see below.

Important accounts of excavations of early historic hill forts elsewhere in Scotland are the following: Alcock L and Alcock E (1987) Reconnaissance excavations on Early Historic fortifications and other royal sites in Scotland, 1974–84: 2, Excavations at Dunollie Castle, Oban, Argyll, 1978 in *PSAS* 117 p 119–47; Alcock L, Alcock E and Driscoll S (1989) Reconnaissance excavations on Early Historic fortifications and other royal sites in Scotland, 1974–84: 3, Dundurn in *PSAS* 119 p 189–226; Alcock L and Alcock E (1987) Reconnaissance excavations on Early Historic fortifications and other royal sites in Scotland, 1974–84: 4, Excavations at Alt Clut, Clyde Rock, Strathclyde, 1974–5 in *PSAS* 120 (1990) p 95–149.

9. Castle Dounie–Argyll 6 no. 285.

10. Ardifuar–Argyll 6 no. 270. Christison D, Anderson J and Ross T (1905) Report of the Society's excavations of forts on the Poltalloch Estate, Argyll, in 1904–5, *PSAS* 39 (1904–5) p 259–70.

11. Duntroon–Argyll 6 no. 257. Christison *et al* (see above n. 10) in *PSAS* 39 (1904–5) p 27–85.

12. Eilean Righ–Argyll 6 no. 320. Brown M and Cowie T (1987) A Dun on Eilean Righ, Loch Craignish, Argyll in *GAJ* 14 (1987) p 58–62.

13. Dùn Chonallaich–Argyll 6 no. 250

14. Dùn na Nighinn–Argyll 6 no. 314.

15. Dunadd–Argyll 6 no. 248 Several campaigns of excavation: Christison D (1904) The forts of Kilmartin, Kilmichael Glassary, and North Knapdale, Argyle, *PSAS* 38 (1903–4) p 205–51; Christison *et al* (see above n. 10) in *PSAS* 39 (1904–5) p 292–322; Craw J H (1930) Excavations at Dunadd and at Other Sites on the Poltalloch Estates, Argyll, in *PSAS* 64 (1929–30) p 111–127. The publication of a full report of the 1980-1 excavations is forthcoming: Lane A and Campbell E (1999) *Excavations at Dunadd–an early Dalriadic capital*, Oxford (Oxbow monograph)

16. Druim an Dùin–Argyll 6 no. 293. Christison (see above n. 15) in *PSAS* 38 (1903-4) p 238–41. Christison *et al* (see above n. 10) in *PSAS* 39 (1904–5) p 285-92.

p 82 DUNADD

17. The earliest accounts of migration from Ireland are found in *Bede's History of the English Church and People*, book 1 ch. 1; Annals of Tigernach (see Anderson A (1990–first published 1922) *Early Sources of Scottish History AD 500 to 1286*, Stamford (originally Edinburgh) vol 1 p 1); Senchus Fer an Alban (see Bannerman J (1974) *Studies in the History of Dalriada*, Edinburgh p 47). The process may have begun earlier, with some population movement (in both directions) accompanying the cultural exchange between Ireland and Western Scotland that is in evidence throughout prehistory. Alternatively there may have been very little population movement at all–at least in a colonial sense–, even after AD 500. See Campbell E (1999–forthcoming) Ireland, Scotland and Wales: archaeology and Celtic regional identity in Driscoll S, Hooper J and Rutherford A (eds) *Expressions of Regional Identity*. Monograph Society for Medieval Archaeology. See also Campbell E (1999) *Saints and Sea-kings: the first kingdom of the Scots*, Edinburgh.

18. Adomnán's *Life of Columba*, Book 1 ch. 28 (p 132 in Sharpe (transl) 1995). Trade is discussed by Campbell E (1996) in Trade in the Dark-Age West: a peripheral activity? in Crawford B (ed) (1996) *Scotland in Dark Age Britain*, Aberdeen. See also a map showing a distribution of pottery imported into Britain AD 400–1000 in McNeill P and MacQueen H (1996) p 57.

19. Campbell E and Lane A (1993) Celtic and Germanic interaction: the 7th century Metalworking Site at Dunadd, in Spearman and Higgitt (1993) *The Age of Migrating Ideas: Early Medieval Art in Northern Britain and Ireland*, Edinburgh.

p 83 KINGS AND SAINTS

20. Argyll 6 no. 248. Argyll 7 no. 281. See Thomas F W L (1879) Dunadd, Glassary, Argyllshire; The Place of Inauguration of the Dalriadic Kings in *PSAS* 13 (1878–9) p 28–47.

21. *Life of Columba*, III.5 (p 208 in Sharpe (transl) 1995). It has been argued that the inauguration may never actually have happened. For a summary of the main points in the debate see Foster S (1996) p 39.

22. See introduction in Sharpe R (transl) (1995) which includes genealogical tables showing Columba's relationship with the heroic figure Niall of the 9 hostages.

23. The poem is given (in Latin and in translation) in Clancy T and Markus G (1995) p 69–80 with full notes.

24. Recent investigations have suggested that the summit area had been altered, possibly to increase visibility of the rituals from below. See Lane A and Campbell E (forthcoming).

25. Campbell E (1987) A cross-marked quern from Dunadd and other evidence for relations between Dunadd and Iona, *PSAS* 117 p 105–117.

p 84 WRITING

26. Ptolemy's 2nd century map gives a p-Celtic name for the tribe inhabiting what is now Kintyre - the Epidii. This suggests a p-Celtic population but does not prove it; much depends on the language spoken by Ptolemy's informant. Ptolemy's map is given in McNeill P and MacQueen H (1996) p 36. A discussion of the derivation of the word Epidii (from Epos - horse) is given in Watson W (1926 & 1993) *The Celtic Placenames of Scotland*, Edinburgh p 23–4 (2nd ed.). Regarding inscriptions the traditional argument that the ogham on Dunadd was in Pictish and unintelligible has been superceded by a reading which shows it is Irish and probably commemorates someone called Finn; see Forsyth K in Lane A and Campbell E (forthcoming).

27. See Clancy T and Markus G (1995) p 209–222 for a listing of books likely to have been in Iona's library.

28. The entries themselves come from the Annals of Ulster, but from the wording, the careful record of Iona abbots, the very precise dating between 686 and 740, and the many references to Scottish forts it has been argued that the compiler used a now lost chronicle from Iona. See Bannerman J (1974) Notes on the Scottish Entries in the Early Irish Annals, in *Studies in the History of Dalriada*, Edinburgh p 9–26 The Dunadd entries are mentioned on p 15.

29. Historians continue attempting to unravel the confusion of evidence. See, for example, Wormald P (1996) The Emergence of the Regnum Scottorum: A Carolingian Hegemony? in Crawford B (ed) (1996) *Scotland in Dark Age Britain*, Aberdeen p 131-153, and Broun D (1998) Pictish Kings 761–839: Integration with Dal Riata or Separate Development? In Foster S (ed) (1998) *The St Andrew Sarcophagus: a Pictish masterpiece and its international connections*, Dublin p 71–83. See also Foster S (1996).

30. The ogham was found in association with long graves in a place formerly known as Kill y Kiaran. See Argyll 7 no. 91. Its discovery is described by Craw in *PSAS* 66 (1931–2) p 448–50.

31. Barnakill. Argyll 6 no. 13.

32. Cella Diuni is mentioned in Adomnán's *Life of Columba* Bkl.Ch31 (Sharpe R (transl) (1995) p 134). For the link with Annat see Clancy T (1995) Annat in Scotland and the origins of the parish, in *Innes Review* vol 46 no. 2 p 91–115.

33. Early Christian monastery, chapel and settlement at Eileach an Naoimh, Garvellachs–Argyll 5 no. 354.

34. The stone comes from Achadh na Cille, Oib at the head of Loch Sween–Argyll 7 no. 2.

FURTHER READING

The most comprehensive guide to the area and period covered in this book is RCAHMS (1999a). An excellent background to the sites mentioned is Ritchie (ed) (1997). The two recent series of titles from Batsford and Canongate give the picture in Scotland as a whole.

Books are listed below for one or more of the following reasons: they deal with sites in the Kilmartin area; they give background information which enhances understanding of Kilmartin's sites; they were used extensively in the writing of the main text of this book and are referred to often in the footnotes. Unfortunately some of the titles are out of print. They are mentioned because they are too important to leave out; all are available in libraries and in some cases re-prints are planned.

Armit I (1998) *Celtic Scotland*, London (Batsford / Historic Scotland series).

Ashmore P J (1996) *Neolithic and Bronze Age Scotland*, London (Batsford / Historic Scotland series).

Bradley R (1997) *Rock Art and the Prehistory of Atlantic Europe*, London.

Campbell E (1999) *Saints and Sea-kings: the first kingdom of the Scots*, Edinburgh (Canongate / Historic Scotland series).

Campbell M and Sandeman M (1962) *Mid Argyll: an archaeological survey*, in *PSAS* 95 p 1–125.

Clancy T O and Markus G (1995) I*ona, the Earliest Poetry of a Celtic Monastery*, Edinburgh.

Clarke D V, Cowie T G and Foxon A (1985) *Symbols of Power at the Time of Stonehenge*, Edinburgh.

Edwards K J and Ralston I B M (eds) (1997) *Scotland – Environment and Archaeology 8000 BC – AD 1000*, Chichester.

Foster S M (1996) *Picts, Gaels and Scots*, London (Batsford / Historic Scotland series).

Lane A and Campbell E (forthcoming) *Excavations at Dunadd: an early Dalriadic capital*, Oxford (Oxbow Monographs).

McNeill P and MacQueen H (eds) (1996) *Atlas of Scottish History to 1707*, Edinburgh.

Mellars P A (1987) *Excavations on Oronsay; Prehistoric Human Ecology on a Small Island*, Edinburgh.

Morris R W B (1977) *The Rock art of Argyll*, Poole.

Morrison I (1985) *Landscape with Lake Dwellings: the crannogs of Scotland*, Edinburgh..

Pollard T and Morrison A (eds) (1996) *The Early Prehistory of Scotland*, Edinburgh.

Ritchie G (ed) (1997) *The Archaeology of Argyll*, Edinburgh.

Royal Commission on the Ancient and Historical Monuments of Scotland (1971) *Argyll: an Inventory of the Ancient Monuments. Vol 1: Kintyre*, Edinburgh.

RCAHMS (1975) *Argyll: an Inventory of the Ancient Monuments. Vol 2: Lorn*, Edinburgh.

RCAHMS (1980) *Argyll: an Inventory of the Ancient Monuments. Vol 3: Mull, Tiree, Coll and Northern Argyll*, Edinburgh.

RCAHMS (1982) *Argyll: an Inventory of the Ancient Monuments. Vol 4: Iona*, Edinburgh.

RCAHMS (1984) *Argyll: an Inventory of the Ancient Monuments. Vol 5: Islay, Jura, Colonsay and Oronsay*, Edinburgh.

RCAHMS (1988) *Argyll: an Inventory of the Ancient Monuments. Vol 6: Mid Argyll and Cowal, Prehistoric and Early Historic Monuments*, Edinburgh.

RCAHMS (1992) *Argyll: an Inventory of the Ancient Monuments. Vol 7: Mid Argyll and Cowal: Medieval and Later Historic monuments*, Edinburgh.

RCAHMS (1997) *Argyll Castles in the Care of Historic Scotland: extracts from RCAHMS inventories vols 1,2 and 7*, Edinburgh.

RCAHMS (1999a) *Kilmartin – Prehistoric and Early Historic Monuments: an inventory of the monuments extracted from Argyll volume 6*, Stationary Office, Edinburgh.

RCAHMS (1999b – forthcoming) *Early Medieval Sculpture in the West Highlands*.

Scott J G (1989) *The Stone circles at Temple Wood, Kilmartin, Argyll*, in *GAJ* 15 p 53–124.

Sharpe R (1995 – transl) *Adomnán of Iona – Life of Columba*, London.

Smith C (1992) *Late Stone Age Hunters of the British Isles*, London.

Smyth A P (1984) *Warlords and Holy Men*, London.

Smout T C (ed) (1993) *Scotland since Prehistory: natural change and human impact*, Aberdeen.

Walker M J C, Gray J M and Lowe J J (eds) (1992) *The South-West Scottish Highlands: Field Guide, Quaternary Research Association*, Cambridge.

Watson W J (1926 – republished 1993) *The History of the Celtic Place-names of Scotland*, Edinburgh.

Wickham-Jones C R (1994) *Scotland's First Settlers*, London (Batsford / Historic Scotland series).

INDEX

Notes: 1. Page numbers in **bold** indicate **location and access** details. Pages in *italics* refer to *captions* to illustrations. There are occasionally textual references on the same pages. 2. Most references are to Kilmartin, which is therefore generally omitted from the index.